Editor
Sara Connolly

Illustrator
Howard Chaney

Cover Artist
Brenda DiAntonis

Managing Editor
Karen J. Goldfluss, M.S. Ed.

Creative Director
Karen J. Goldfluss, M.S. Ed.

Art Production Manager
Kevin Barnes

Art Coordinator
Renée Christine Yates

Imaging
Denise Thomas
James Edward Grace
Nathan Rivera

Publisher
Mary D. Smith, M.S. Ed.

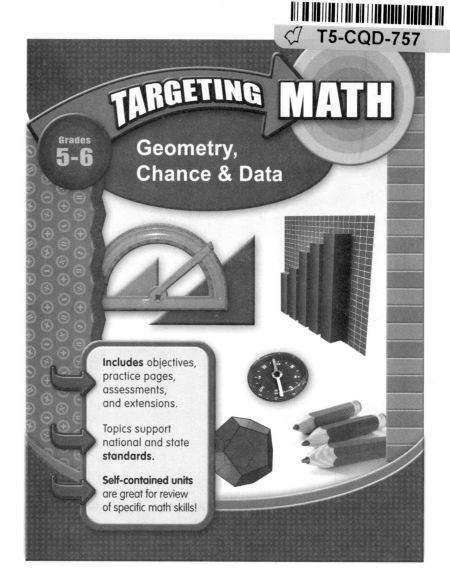

T5-CQD-757

TARGETING MATH

Grades 5-6

Geometry, Chance & Data

Includes objectives, practice pages, assessments, and extensions.

Topics support national and state **standards.**

Self-contained units are great for review of specific math skills!

Authors

Gloria Harris, Garda Turner, Kerry Walker, Nicole Bauer, and Dona Martin

(Revised and Rewritten by Teacher Created Resources, Inc.)

Teacher Created Resources, Inc.
6421 Industry Way
Westminster, CA 92683
www.teachercreated.com
ISBN-13: 978-1-4206-8999-0
© 2007 Teacher Created Resources, Inc.
Made in U.S.A.

Teacher Created Resources

Table of Contents

© *Teacher Created Resources, Inc.*

Table of Contents

#8999 Targeting Math: Geometry, Chance, and Data

Introduction

Targeting Math

The Targeting Math Series is a comprehensive classroom resource. It has been developed so that teachers can find activities and reproducible pages for all areas of the primary math curriculum.

About This Series

The twelve books in the series cover all aspects of the math curriculum in an easy-to-read format. Each level—grades 1 and 2, grades 3 and 4, and grades 5 and 6—has four books: *Numeration* and *Fractions; Operations and Number Patterns; Geometry, Chance, and Data;* and *Measurement.* Each topic in a book is covered by one or more units that are progressive in level. You will be able to find resources for each student, whatever his or her ability may be. This enables you to accommodate different ability groups within your class. It also allows you to quickly find worksheets at different levels for remediation and extension.

About This Book

Targeting Math: Geometry, Chance, and Data (Grades 5 and 6) contains topics covering Three-Dimensional Shapes; Two-Dimensional Shapes; Position, Mapping, and Transformation; and Chance and Data. Each topic is covered by one to three complete units of work. (See Table of Contents for specific skills.)

About Each Unit

Each unit is complete within itself. It begins with a list of objectives, resources needed, mathematical language used, and a description of each reproducible. This is followed by suggested student activities to reinforce learning. The reproducible pages cover different aspects of the topic in a progressive nature and all answers are included. Every unit includes an assessment page. These assessment pages are important resources in themselves as teachers can use them to find out what their students know about a new topic. They can also be used for assessing specific outcomes when clear feedback is needed.

About the Skills Index

A Skills Index is provided at the end of the book. It lists specific objectives for the student pages of each unit of the book.

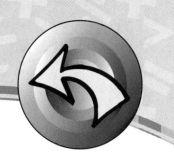

THREE-DIMENSIONAL SHAPES

These units provide opportunities to draw, model, classify, and name three-dimensional shapes. Students identify prisms, pyramids, cones, cylinders and spheres. They identify and count faces, edges, and vertices. They also model, draw, and describe regular shapes.

Students build models of irregular shapes from drawings and then draw them on isometric dot paper. They identify and draw cross-sections of everyday objects and relate regular three-dimensional shapes to real life and their surroundings.

The activity page displays some interesting unfolded figures. The students use these to build the five platonic solids.

Two assessment pages are included.

5

THREE-DIMENSIONAL SHAPES

Unit 1

Prisms
Pyramids
Building Three-
Dimensional Solids
Drawing Three-
Dimensional Solids

Objectives

- recognize three-dimensional objects
- describe three-dimensional objects
- make and represent three-dimensional objects
- identify prisms and pyramids from drawings
- describe and compare faces, edges, and vertices of prisms and pyramids
- make complex models from visual information
- represent three-dimensional shapes by drawing models

Language

prism, pyramid, cube, edge, vertex, vertices, triangular, rectangular, pentagonal, hexagonal, octagonal, model corresponding, parallelogram

Materials/Resources

multilink cubes, isometric dot paper, blank paper, models of prisms and pyramids, rulers

Contents of Student Pages

* *Materials needed for each reproducible student page*

Page 8 Prisms
names of prisms; counting edges, vertices, faces

* *models of prisms*

Page 9 Pyramids
names of pyramids; counting edges, faces, vertices

* *models of pyramids*

Page 10 Drawing Shapes
* *blank paper—2 sheets per student, rulers*

Page 11 Identifying Shapes
identifying prisms and pyramids from written descriptions; writing descriptions for given models

Page 12 Modeling Shapes
modeling prisms from drawings; drawing prisms from models.

* *multilink cubes (20 per student), isometric dot paper (2 sheets per student)*

Page 13 More Modeling Shapes
creating prisms from models; estimating multilinks needed; counting multilinks used

* *45 multilink cubes for each student*

Page 14 Assessment
Page 15 Activity Page

Remember

Before starting, ensure that each student:

- ❑ *understands that all straight lines must be ruled*
- ❑ *knows the adjectival form of shape names—e.g., triangular, pentagonal*

Additional Activities

❑ Have students explore school surroundings for three-dimensional shapes. They can draw the shapes and record names.

❑ Students can design a house using prisms and pyramids on isometric dot paper.

❑ Have students work in pairs to make models of prisms and pyramids from a variety of materials.

❑ Cut out six squares. Have students arrange them in various ways to make different unfolded figures for a cube.

❑ Make a class chart to show examples of tri, quad, hex, poly, etc.

Answers

Page 8 Prisms

a. Triangular prism	5	9	6
b. Pentagonal prism	7	15	10
c. Cube	6	12	8
d. Rectangular prism	6	12	8
e. Octagonal prism	10	24	16
f. Hexagonal prism (octahedron)	8	18	12

Page 9 Pyramids

1. Check individual work.
2.

a. Triangular pyramid (Tetrahedron)	4	6	4
b. Pentagonal pyramid	6	10	6
c. Square pyramid	5	8	5
d. Hexagonal pyramid	7	12	7
e. Rectangular pyramid	5	8	5
f. Octagonal pyramid	9	16	9

Page 10 Drawing Shapes

Check individual work.

Page 11 Identifying Shapes

1. a. Rectangular pyramid
   b. Triangular prism
   c. Pentagonal pyramid
   d. Hexagonal prism
   e. Triangular pyramid—tetrahedron
2. Check individual work.

Page 12 Modeling Shapes

1. Check individual work.
2. a. yes
   b. d and e, 13 cubes

Page 13 More Modeling Shapes

1. a. 6
   b. 16
   c. 6
   d. 40
   e. 25
2. 42

Page 14 Assessment

1. Check individual work.
2. a. Pentagonal pyramid
   b. 6
   c. 10
   d. 6
3. Check individual work.
4. A prism has mainly rectangular faces and two bases; a pyramid has mainly triangular faces and one base.
5. Check individual work.
6. A solid shape which has 2 hexagonal ends joined by 6 rectangular faces.

Page 15 Activity Page

Check individual work.

| **Name** | **Date** |

Fill in the table by looking at the pictures.

A

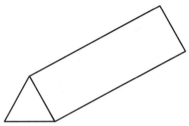

B

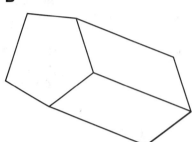

C

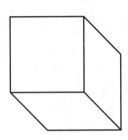

D

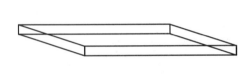

E

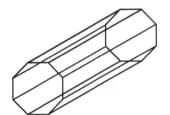

F

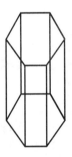

Model	Name	Number of Faces	Number of Edges	Number of Vertices
A				
B				
C				
D				
E				
F				

(8)

Name	Date

1. Explain how a pyramid differs from a prism. _____

_____

2. Fill in the table by looking at the pictures. C and F are views from the top.

A

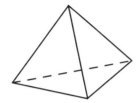

B

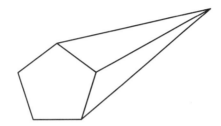

C

D

E

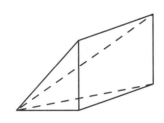

F

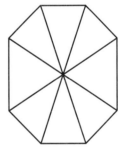

Model	Name	Number of Faces	Number of Edges	Number of Vertices
A				
B				
C				
D				
E				
F				

⑨

Name	**Date**

Practice drawing prisms and pyramids by following the instructions.

1. Trace over the dotted lines. Remember to use a ruler and a sharp pencil.

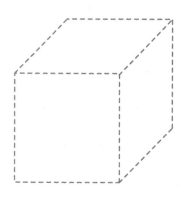 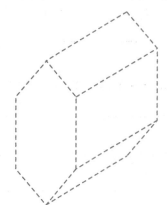 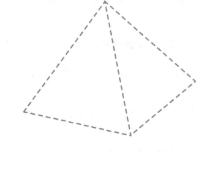

2. **a.** Draw one rectangle. Then draw an identical rectangle below and a little to the right of the first.

   b. Connect the corresponding vertices.

   c. Try your own.

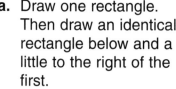

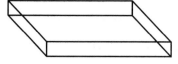

3. **a.** Draw a parallelogram.

   b. Put a dot above the parallelogram and connect each vertex to it.

   c. Try your own.

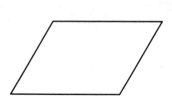

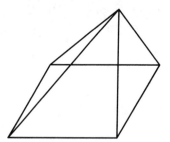

4. You now have an easy way of drawing prisms and pyramids. On your own paper, practice drawing:

   a. a square pyramid

   b. a pentagonal prism

   c. a triangular pyramid (tetrahedron)

   d. an octagonal prism

10

| **Name** | **Date** |

1. On the back of this paper, draw and name each solid.

a. I have one rectangular face and my other faces are triangles. I also have five corners.
b. I have three rectangular faces and two equilateral triangular faces.
c. I have six vertices and 10 edges. One of my faces is a regular pentagon.
d. I have eight faces, and 12 vertices. Two of my faces are hexagons.
e. I have two common names. I am made of four congruent shapes and have four vertices.

2. Write a clear description of each solid. Discuss your description with a partner.

   a.

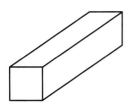

_____

_____

_____

   b.

_____

_____

_____

   c.

_____

_____

_____

   d.

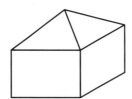

_____

_____

_____

11

Name	**Date**

You will need 20 multilink cubes and isometric dot paper.

1. Model these shapes. Draw each model on isometric dot paper. If your drawing looks strange (as many do the first time), try again.

a. 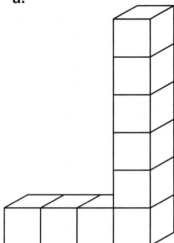   **b.** 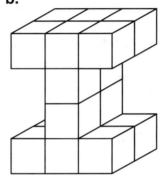   **c.**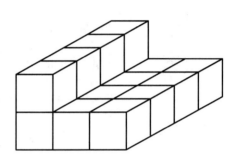

d. 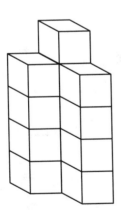   **e.**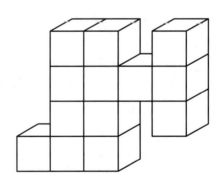

2. **a.** Are any models made from the same number of multilinks?

_____

    b. If so, which ones and how many multilink cubes?

_____

(12)

Name	**Date**

You will need 45 multilink cubes.

1. Using multilinks, model these shapes. Before you start, estimate how many blocks you think you will use. When you have finished, count how many you did use.

   a.

   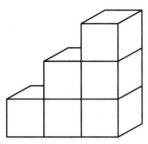

   Estimate_____

   Actual_____

   b.

   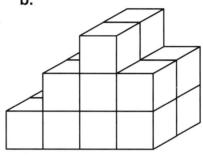

   Estimate_____

   Actual_____

   c.

   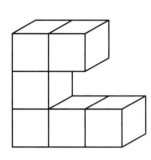

   Estimate_____

   Actual_____

   d.

   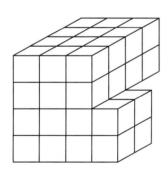

   Estimate_____

   Actual_____

   e.

   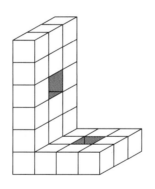

   Estimate_____

   Actual_____

2. Now for a much harder example. Can you do it?

   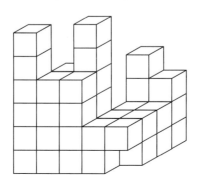

   Estimate_____

   Actual_____

(13)

Name	**Date**

1. You will need a ruler and a sharp pencil. In the space below draw a triangular prism.

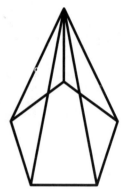

2. **a.** Name this solid shape. _____

    b. How many faces does it have? _____

    c. How many edges does it have? _____

    d. How many vertices does it have? _____

3. Repeat this drawing in the space beside it.

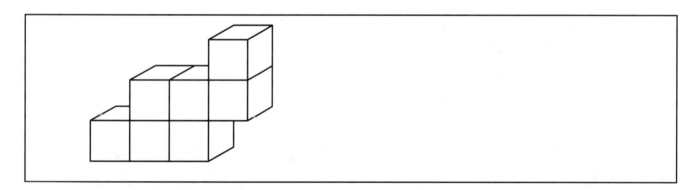

4. What is the main difference between a prism and a pyramid?

_____

_____

_____

5. Draw the top view of a square pyramid.

6. Write a clear description of a hexagonal prism.

_____

_____

_____

_____

(14)

Name	Date

Interesting Unfolded Figures

Make these platonic solids. You will have to enlarge and draw their unfolded figures from the diagrams given. You may wish to make the solids from Polydron pieces first.

Tetrahedron

Cube

Octahedron

Dodecahedron

Icosahedron

When you have finished, make a grid showing how many faces, edges and vertices each solid has.

THREE-DIMENSIONAL SHAPES

Unit 2

Cylinders
Cones
Spheres
Drawing Three-
Dimensional Solids

Objectives

- draw recognizable cylinders, cones, and spheres
- sketch elevations of cones, cylinders, and spheres
- list properties of cones, cylinders, and spheres
- select figures that meet criteria related to sides, faces, and vertices
- recognize an object from different view points
- discuss packing properties of three-dimensional objects
- investigate and describe cross-sections of three-dimensional shapes

Language

cone, conical, cylinder, cylindrical, sphere, spherical, net, edge, vertex, vertices, cross-section, ellipse, view

Materials/Resources

models of cylinders, cones, spheres, scissors, sticky tape, blank sheets of paper, modeling clay, colored pencils

Contents of Student Pages

* *Materials needed for each reproducible student page*

....
Remember

Before starting, ensure that each student:

- ☐ *understands the need to use a ruler to draw all straight lines*
- ☐ *knows the language for spheres, cones, and cylinders*

Additional Activities

❑ *Have students explore school surroundings for conical, spherical, and cylindrical shapes.*

❑ *Have students gather pictures from magazines, newspapers, etc. which show the shapes of cones, cylinders, and spheres in everyday life. Make three wall charts.*

❑ *Have students design an interesting piece of furniture using only cones or cylinders or spheres—then discuss the designs as a class.*

❑ *Divide the class into four groups. Give each group (or have them make) models of one shape. They can then pack the models into a carton. Have the whole class meet to discuss the success/difficulty of the task.*

❑ *Have students work in groups of three or four. Give each group a selection of cones, spheres, and cylinders. Have them investigate rolling the models and write reports on their findings.*

❑ *Give students models of cones, cylinders, and spheres. Have students work in groups of three or four to wrap the models in newspaper as presents. Then have a whole-class discussion on the ease/difficulty of the task.*

Answers
Page 18 Cones, Cylinders, and Spheres

1. a.	Cone	2	1	0
b.	Sphere	1	0	0
c.	Cylinder	3	2	0

2. Check individual work.
3. Check individual work.

Page 19 Shapes in Everyday Life

1. a. sphere
   b. cone
   c. cone
   d. sphere
   e. cylinder
   f. cylinder
2. Check individual work.
3. a. b. c.

   d. e. f.

4. a. Paper roll or cheese—will have less gaps so everything fits together easily.
   b. Cone or party hat—the shape will leave large gaps and the items will not stack on one another.

Page 20 Cross-Sections
1.

   a. b. c.

   d. e. f.

   g. h. i.

2.–3. Check individual work.

Page 21 Views of Three-Dimensional Shapes
Check individual work.

Page 22 Assessment

1. a. cone
   b. 2
   c.
2. cylinder
3. a. Check individual work.
   b. A sphere does not have flat faces.
4. a. b. c.

#8999 Targeting Math: Geometry, Chance, and Data

Name	**Date**

You will need colored pencils, scissors, and tape for this activity.

Remember:
- A **Face** is a flat surface.
- An **Edge** is where two faces meet.
- A **Vertex** is where two or more edges meet.

---

1. Work with a partner. Discuss each model before you write your answers.

	Model	Name	Number of Faces	Number of Edges	Number of Vertices
A					
B					
C					

2. These are the unfolded figures of a cone and a cylinder. Draw a pattern on each before cutting them out. Assemble them carefully using tape.

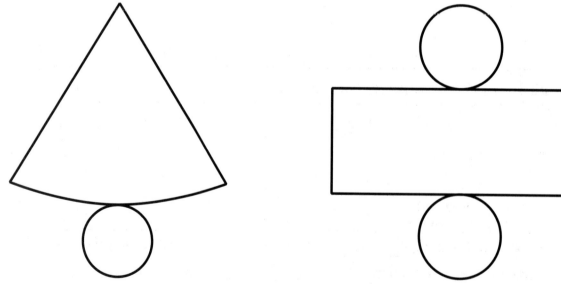

3. Explain why we do not have an unfolded figure for a sphere._____

_____

#8999 Targeting Math: Geometry, Chance, and Data   © *Teacher Created Resources, Inc.*

Name	**Date**

1. Name the shape of each.

   a.   **b.**    **c.**

   _____   _____   _____

   d.    **e.** 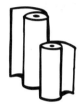   **f.**

   _____   _____   _____

2. Think of some more everyday items which have the shape of a cone, a cylinder, and a sphere. Draw two items of each shape. Ask a classmate if he/she can recognize them.

Cone	**Sphere**	**Cylinder**

3. Draw the view from the top of each item in Question 1.

a.	**b.**	**c.**	**d.**	**e.**	**f.**

4. If you were packing the items in Question 1 into a box, which would be

   a. easiest to pack and why? _____

   b. hardest to pack and why? _____

Name	**Date**

You will need some blank paper.

1. Draw the shape of each cross-section.

   a.   **b.**    **c.**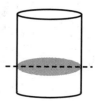

   d. 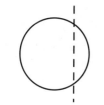   **e.** 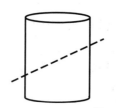   **f.**

   g.    **h.**    **i.**

If you find this difficult, model the shapes using modeling clay first.

2. Draw each shape following the instructions.

Sphere
   a. Draw a circle.
   b. Shade one side to indicate that it is solid.

Cone
   a. Draw an ellipse (oval).
   b. Mark a point above the ellipse.
   c. Join the sides of the ellipse to the point.

Cylinder
   a. Draw an ellipse.
   b. Draw the sides vertically downward from the ellipse.
   c. Join the bottom of the sides with a curve to match top edge.

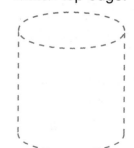

3. On a blank piece of paper draw your own cones, spheres, and cylinders.

Name		**Date**

1. These are some everyday objects.

a.  b.  c.  d.

Name each and then draw what it looks like from the front, the top and the bottom.

	Name	**View from front**	**View from top**	**View from bottom**
a.				
b.				
c.				
d.				

2. Draw a chair, a skateboard, a milk carton, and a pear. On the back of this page, create a table like the one in Question 1 and draw the side view, the top view, and the front view of each object.

21

Name	**Date**

1. **a.** Name this shape _____

   b. How many faces does it have?

   _____

   c. Draw the shapes of its faces.

2. What three-dimensional solid would this unfolded figure make?

   _____

3. **a.** Draw a sphere.

   b. Why don't we have an unfolded figure for a sphere?

   _____

   _____

   _____

   _____

   _____

   _____

4. Draw the top view of these everyday items.

   a.    **b.**   **c.**

Name   **Date**

#8999 Targeting Math: Geometry, Chance, and Data

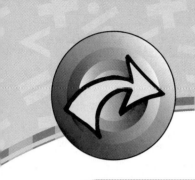

TWO-DIMENSIONAL SHAPES

There are three units in this topic. The first unit deals with angles. Students name angles according to type and size. They use protractors to measure degrees and to draw angles of given sizes. They practice drawing reflex angles and find the sum of the angles of triangles.

In the second and third units, students name and draw regular and irregular polygons. They identify special quadrilaterals and work out the angle sum of quadrilaterals. They name triangles according to the lengths of sides and label the parts of circles.

Students use horizontal, vertical, and parallel lines to make patterns. They use a pair of compasses to draw circles and to construct triangles. They draw quadrilaterals using protractors and parallel lines.

There are three assessment pages and one activity page. The activity page encourages students to draw spirals using a pair of compasses.

24

TWO-DIMENSIONAL SHAPES

Unit 1

Types of Angles
Angle Sums
Drawing Angles
Measuring Angles

Objectives

- use degrees as a formal unit
- construct angles using a protractor
- read scales to the nearest measurement mark
- use conventional units and measuring equipment for angles
- make sensible estimates of size
- examine properties of triangles and quadrilaterals
- classify angles according to size

Language

angle, acute, obtuse, reflex, revolution, protractor, vertex, rays

Materials/Resources

protractors, scissors, blank paper

Contents of Student Pages

. . . .
Remember

Before starting, ensure that each student:

☐ clearly understands which line of numbers should be read on a protractor

☐ has a ruler

25

Additional Activities

❏ *Have students work in pairs. One student draws an angle, both students estimate its size, and then one measures it. The closest estimate scores a point. Have them take turns to draw and measure. The first person to get 5 points wins.*

❏ *Have students find examples of each type of angle in the classroom and on the playground.*

❏ *Have students make their own protractors.*

❏ *Students can write a step by step guide to using a protractor. They can ask partners to act out the steps to see if the guide works.*

Answers

Page 27 Types of Angles
1. <RDY or < YDR acute
2. <NUT or <TUN obtuse
3. <XYZ or <ZYX right angle
4. <CAT or <TAC reflex
5. <NEB or <BEN straight angle
6. <FUN or <NUF obtuse
7. <LML revolution
8. <PRT or <TRP right angle
9. <FGH or <HGF acute

Page 28 Measuring Angles
1. Acute 40°
2. Right 90°
3. Obtuse 130°
4. Straight 180°
5. Acute 22°
6. Obtuse 99°
7. Obtuse 117°
8. Acute 85°
9. Right 90°

Page 29 Measuring Reflex Angles
1. 250°
2. 220°
3. 360°
4. 310°
5. 315°
6. 270°
7. 188°
8. 214°

Page 30 Drawing Angles
Check individual work.

Page 31 Drawing Reflex Angles
Check individual work.

Page 32 Sum of Angles
1. a. 180°
   b. yes
2. Check individual work.
3. The edges make a straight angle. The sum of the three angles in a triangle is 180.

Page 33 Assessment
1. a. <MNP or <PNM reflex
   b. <DLT or <TLD straight
   c. <ABX or <XBA acute
2. a. 27°
   b. 90°
   c. 220°
3. Check individual work.
4. The sum is 180°

Name	**Date**

There are six types of angles.

Acute angles are smaller than 90°.

Obtuse angles are between 90° and 180°.

Reflex angles are between 180° and 360°

Right angles are 90°.

Straight angles are 180°.

Revolutions are 360°.

Naming Angles
Use three letters for each angle. The letter at the vertex
always goes in the middle and < is used for the angle sign.

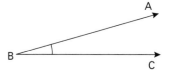

For example, Name <u>*<ABC or <CBA*</u>

Type <u>*acute*</u>

1.
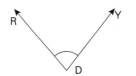

Name _____

Type _____

2.
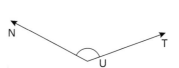

Name _____

Type _____

3.

Name _____

Type _____

4.
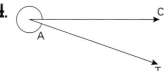

Name _____

Type _____

5.

Name _____

Type _____

6.
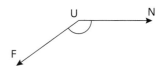

Name _____

Type _____

7.

Name _____

Type _____

8.
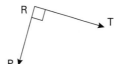

Name _____

Type _____

9.
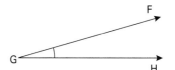

Name _____

Type _____

27

Name	**Date**

You will need a protractor for this activity.

> When you measure an angle, always estimate first. If you know the approximate size (e.g., if it's obtuse you know it must be between 90° and 180°) you will be more likely to read the numbers correctly on your protractor.
>
> If an angle is too small for you to measure, you might need to carefully extend one arm of the angle to make measuring easier. Make sure you use your ruler and a sharp pencil for this.

Write the type and the size of each of the angles below.

1.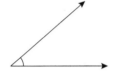

Type _____

Size _____

2.

Type _____

Size _____

3.

Type _____

Size _____

4.

Type _____

Size _____

5.

Type _____

Size _____

6.

Type _____

Size _____

7.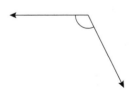

Type _____

Size _____

8.

Type _____

Size _____

9.

Type _____

Size _____

Name	**Date**

You will need a protractor for this activity.

Measuring reflex angles looks like it might be harder than measuring acute or obtuse angles because reflex angles are larger than 180°. Here is a tip that will help you. If you have to measure this angle:

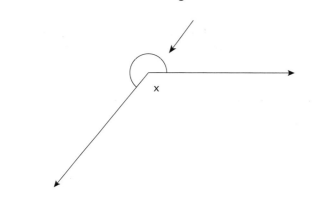

a. Turn your page upside down.

b. Measure the other side of the angle (the part marked with an x). That measures 130°.

c. Angles around a point total 360°, so subtract 130° from 360° (360°−130° = 230°).

d. The angle measures 230°.

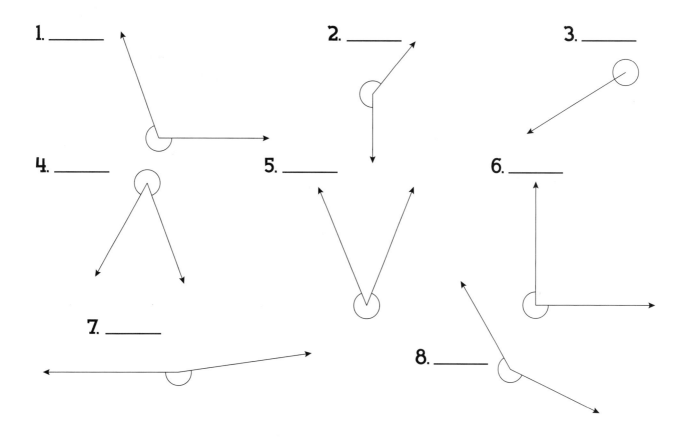

1. _____

2. _____

3. _____

4. _____

5. _____

6. _____

7. _____

8. _____

Name	**Date**

You will need a protractor and a sharp pencil for this activity.

> Before you start to draw an angle, it might help you to picture the type of angle it is in your mind so you have a rough idea of what it should look like.

With A as the vertex, draw these angles. Remember that you can turn your page around if it helps you.

1.
A 30°

2.
90° A

3.
A
100°

4.
A
136°

5.
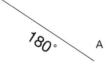
180° A

6.
A 68°

7.

A 153°

8.
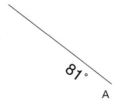
81°
A

30

Name　　　　　　　　　　　**Date**

You will need a protractor for this activity.

Drawing reflex angles is easy once you know the trick.

Follow this example.

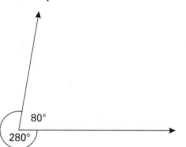

To draw an angle of 280° :

  a. Subtract 280° from 360°. The answer is 80°.

  b. Draw an 80° angle.

  c. The other side of the angle will then be 280°.

On this sheet, draw these angles. Work with a partner. When you have both finished, swap sheets and check each other's angles. Discuss any errors you find.

1. 270°　　　　　　　**4.** 216°

2. 190°　　　　　　　**5.** 321°

3. 305°

31

Name	**Date**

You will need a protractor and a pair of scissors for this activity. Work with a partner.

1. In each triangle below, measure the three interior angles.

    a. What is the sum of these angles? _____

    b. Is this the same for both triangles? _____

2. **a.** Cut out the two triangles.

    b. Tear off the corners of one triangle.

    c. Place all the corners together at a point.

    For example:

    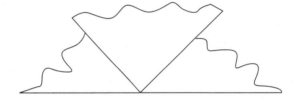

    d. Repeat for the second triangle.

3. What do you notice? _____
   Can you write a rule? _____

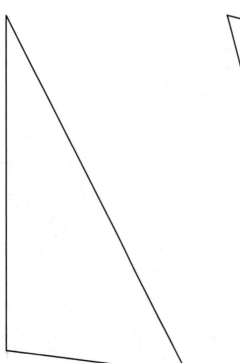

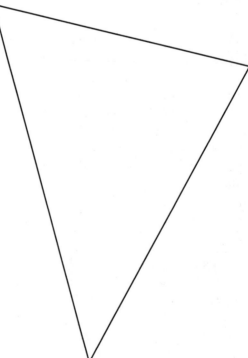

Name	**Date**

1. Name each angle and state its type.

a.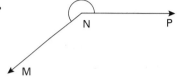

b.

c.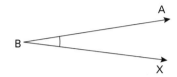

Name _____   Name _____   Name _____

Type _____   Type _____   Type _____

2. Measure these angles.

  a. _____   **b.** _____   **c.** _____

3. Draw these angles.

  a. 105°   **b.** 180°   **c.** 310°

4. Draw a triangle. Measure each angle and write its size. What is the sum of the angles? Write your total in the center of the triangle.

#8999 Targeting Math: Geometry, Chance, and Data

Name   **Date**

You will need a ruler, a sharp pencil, and a pair of compasses for this activity.

- Draw a line across your page and mark two points A and B. These are going to be the two centers you use to draw all the semicircles.

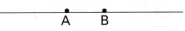

- Put the point of your compass on A, make the radius AB, and draw a semicircle.

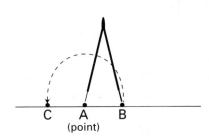

- Put the point of your compass on B, make the radius BC, and draw another semicircle starting from the end of the previous one.

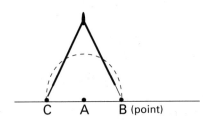

- Using center A and starting from the end of the second semicircle, continue the process.

A Spiral with Four Centers

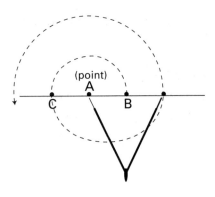

You can draw a spiral with four centers by drawing quarter circles using the corners of the square A, B, C, D, A, B. . . in succession. Try it on another piece of paper.

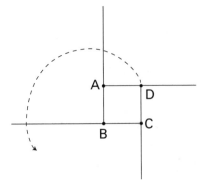

TWO-DIMENSIONAL SHAPES

Unit 2

Quadrilaterals
Triangles
Circles

Objectives

- examine properties of quadrilaterals
- examine properties of triangles
- use geometric tools to interpret and meet specifications
- select figures that meet criteria
- classify polygons and other two-dimensional shapes
- describe and compare properties of two-dimensional shapes
- use conventional language associated with circles

Language

triangle, quadrilateral, pentagon, hexagon, heptagon, octagon, nonagon, decagon, polygon, scalene, isosceles, equilateral, right triangle, radius, diameter, center, arc, circumference, chord, segment, sector, protractor

Materials/Resources

protractors, paper, colored pencils, scissors, red and blue counters

Contents of Student Pages

* *Materials needed for each reproducible student page*

Page 37 Polygons
naming polygons; regular and irregular; drawing polygons

Page 38 Quadrilaterals
special quadrilaterals; naming and drawing special quadrilaterals; square, rectangle, parallelogram, rhombus, kite, trapezoid

Page 39 Angles in Quadrilaterals
angle sum of a quadrilateral

* *protractor, scissors, spear paper*

Page 40 Triangles
names according to length of sides; scalene, isosceles, equilateral, right triangle

* *protractor*

Page 41 Angles in Triangles
names according to size of angles; scalene, isosceles, equilateral, right triangle

* *protractor*

Page 42 Circles
naming part of a circle; center, radius, diameter, chord, arc, circumference, sector, segment, semicircle

* *colored pencils*

Page 43 Assessment
Page 44 Activity Page

Remember

Before starting, ensure that each student:

- ❏ *knows how to use a protractor*
- ❏ *has a protractor to use*
- ❏ *understands that all straight lines must be ruled*
- ❏ *has access to a dictionary or math dictionary*

Additional Activities

❑ *Have students make lists of all quadrilaterals in the classroom.*

❑ *Have students make lists of all polygons that can be seen in the playground.*

❑ *Have students design their bedroom furniture using plane shapes other than squares or rectangles.*

❑ *Students can use tangrams to make as many different rectangles and squares as possible.*

❑ *Students can make five-pieces tangrams starting with a circle.*

❑ *Have students draw shapes inside shapes, for example—a square inside a triangle inside a rectangle, etc.*

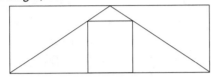

❑ *Make cookies of different shapes and have students identify them.*

Answers

Page 37 Polygons

1. a. pentagon, irregular
   b. hexagon, irregular
   c. octagon, regular
   d. triangle, regular
   e. trapezoid (or quadrilateral) irregular
   f. nonagon, irregular
2. Check individual work.

Page 38 Quadrilaterals

1. Check individual work.
2. Check individual work.
3. a. rhombus
   b. trapezoid
   c. parallelogram
   d. square
   e. kite

Page 39 Angles in Quadrilaterals

1. a. 43°, 118°, 59°, 140°, sum = 360°
   b. 52°, 128°, 98°, 82°, sum—360°
2. The angle sum of a quadrilateral is 360°
3. Check individual work.

Page 40 Triangles

1. a. equilateral
   b. isosceles
   c. scalene
   d. scalene
   e. equilateral
   f. scalene
   g. isosceles
   h. isosceles
2. Check individual work.

Page 41 Angles in Triangles

1. a. scalene, 30°, 80°, 70°
   b. isosceles, 30°, 70°, 80°
   c. equilateral, 60°, 60°, 60°
   d. isosceles, 70°, 70°, 40°
   e. scalene, 50°, 30°, 100°
   f. right 90°, 45°, 45°
2. Check individual work.

Page 42 Circles

1. a. H
   b. MN
   c. MH or HN or HS or HT or GH
   d. AB
   e. Check individual work.
   f. Check individual work.
   g. Check individual work.
2. Check individual work.

Page 43 Assessment

1. a. pentagon
   b. decagon
   c. scalene
   d. trapezoid
   e. semicircle
2. a. kite
   b. hexagon
   c. equilateral triangle
   d. parallelogram
3. Check individual work.
4. All sides are equal, all angles are equal.
5. a. X
   b. XF or XE
   c. FE
   d. AB or BC or CE or ED or DF or FA
   e. Check individual work.
   f. Check individual work.

36

Name	**Date**

Many shape names identify how many sides and angles the shapes have. It is useful to learn these.

triangle	– 3 sides
quadrilateral	– 4 sides
pentagon	– 5 sides
hexagon	– 6 sides
septagon	– 7 sides
octagon	– 8 sides
nonagon	– 9 sides
decagon	– 10 sides

Shapes can be **regular** – which means all the sides are equal and all the angles are equal.

 **square**   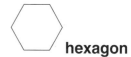 **hexagon**

Irregular shapes – sides are different lengths and the angles are different sizes.

1. Write each figure's name and whether it is regular or irregular.

a.   _____

b.   _____

c.   _____

d.   _____

e.  _____

f. 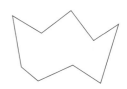 _____

2. Draw:

a. a regular quadrilateral   b. an irregular octagon   c. a regular hexagon

37

Name	**Date**

There are many special quadrilaterals, such as a square and a rectangle. You can sometimes confuse people by saying a square is a rectangle but a rectangle is not a square. Think about it!

1. Write a definition for each shape.

   a. Square _____

   _____

   b. Rectangle _____

   _____

   c. Parallelogram _____

   _____

   d. Rhombus _____

   _____

   e. Kite _____

   _____

   f. Trapezoid _____

   _____

2. Draw an example of each shape in Question 1.

3. Name these shapes.

   a.  **b.**   **c.** 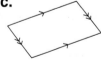 **d.**   **e.**

   _____   _____   _____   _____   _____

#8999 Targeting Math: Geometry, Chance, and Data

© *Teacher Created Resources, Inc.*

Name	**Date**

You will need a protractor, spare paper, and a pair of scissors for this activity.

1. Measure the angles in each quadrilateral. Write the size inside each angle. Find the sum of the angles for each quadrilateral and write it on the line below.

   a.

   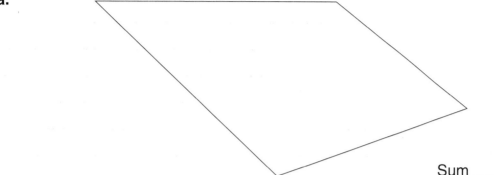

   Sum _____

   b.

   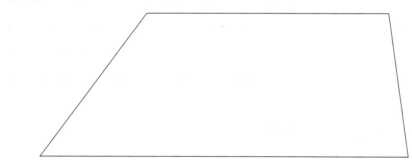

   Sum _____

2. Write a rule for the angle sum of a quadrilateral.

   _____

3. On a piece of paper, draw a large quadrilateral.
   Cut it out.

   Tear off the corners.

   Place all the vertices together at a point.

What happens? _____

_____

Name	**Date**

Triangles have three sides and three angles. Some have special names.

Scalene triangle—all three sides are different lengths.

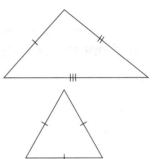

Equilateral triangle—all three sides are the same length.

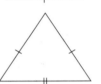

Isosceles triangle—two sides are the same length.

1. Measure the sides of each triangle and write the triangle's name on the line below it.

   a.

   b.

   c.

   d.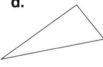

   _____   _____   _____   _____

   e.

   f.

   g.

   h.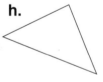

   _____   _____   _____   _____

2. Draw one triangle of each type. Swap with a partner and ask him or her to label each one.

   a.   **b.**   **c.**

#8999 Targeting Math: Geometry, Chance, and Data   © *Teacher Created Resources, Inc.*

Name	**Date**

You will need a protractor for this activity.

Triangles are sometimes named according to the sizes of their angles.

Scalene triangle –
all angles are
different sizes.
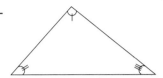

Equilateral triangle –
three angles are equal.
They are always 60˚.

Isosceles triangle –
two angles are equal.
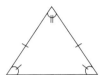

Right-angled triangle –
one angle is a right angle.
It is always 90°.

1 Measure the angles in each triangle. Write the size in each angle and
write the triangle's name.

a.

b.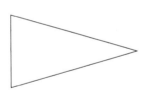

c.

d.

e.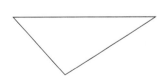

f.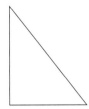

2 Using your protractor, draw
a right-angled isosceles triangle.

41

Name	Date

You will need colored pencils for this activity.

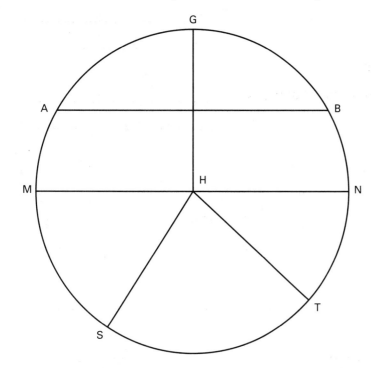

1. Write the letters which show:

   a. the center _____

   b. the diameter _____

   c. a radius _____

   d. a chord _____

   Color:

   e. a blue semicircle

   f. a red arc

   g. a green sector

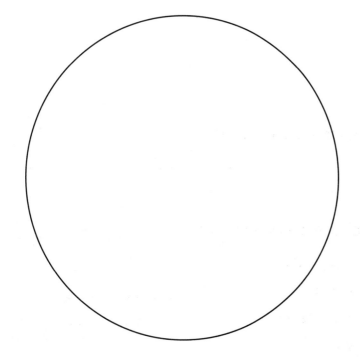

2. On this circle, mark and name:

   a. the center _____

   b. the circumference _____

   c. a chord _____

   d. an arc _____

   e. a radius _____

   f. a segment _____

Name	**Date**

1. What do we call:

   a. a five-sided figure?   _____

   b. a ten-sided figure?   _____

   c. a triangle which has no sides equal?   _____

   d. a four-sided figure with only one pair of parallel sides?   _____

   e. half a circle?   _____

2. Name these figures.

   a. 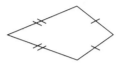   **b.**   **c.**   **d.**

   _____   _____   _____   _____

3. Draw these shapes.

   a. isosceles triangle   **b.** rectangle   **c.** pentagon

4. What does "regular" mean when referring to a plane shape?

   _____

5.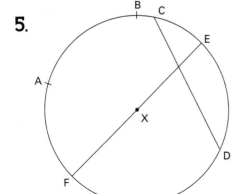

   Write the letters which show:

   a. the center   _____

   b. a radius   _____

   c. a diameter   _____

   d. an arc   _____

   e. Shade a semicircle.

   f. Draw stripes in a segment.

43

#8999 Targeting Math: Geometry, Chance, and Data

Name

Date

You will need three red counters and three blue counters.

Place them on the playing board like this.

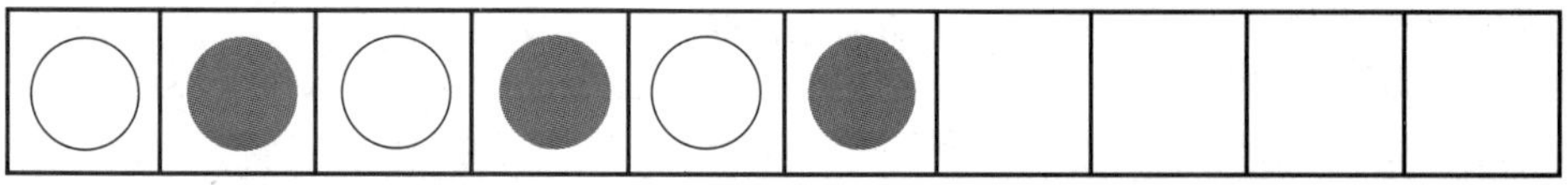

Your aim is to get all the red counters together and all the blue counters together like this.

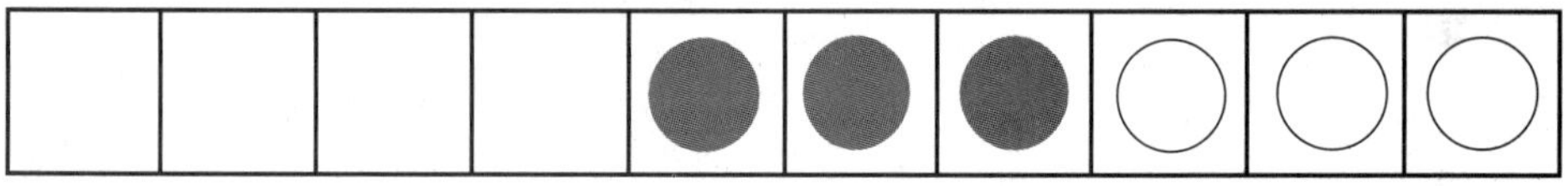

Each turn you must move two counters that are next to each other without changing their order.

For Example,

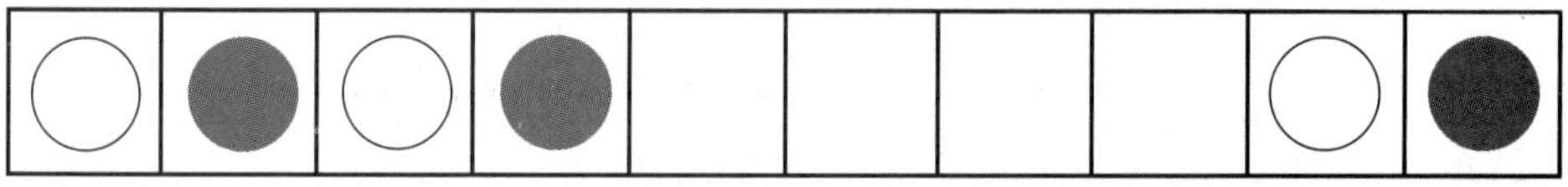

Like this…

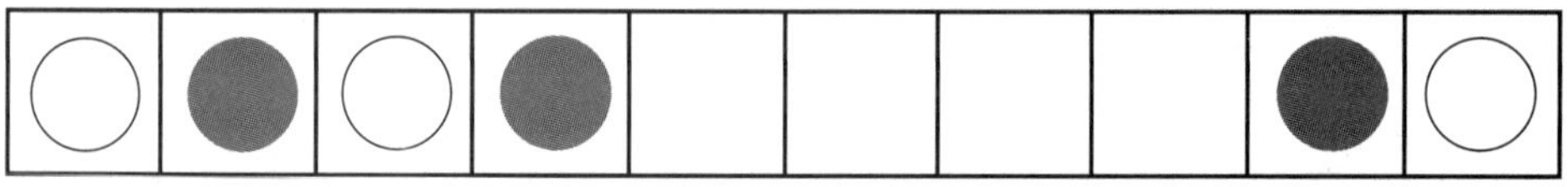

not like this.

Challenge

Change

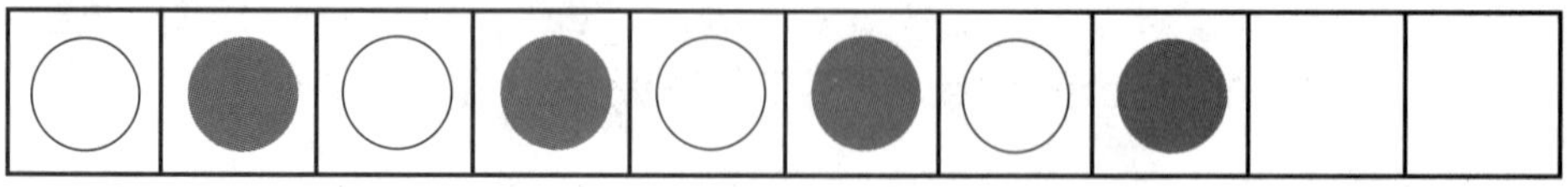

to

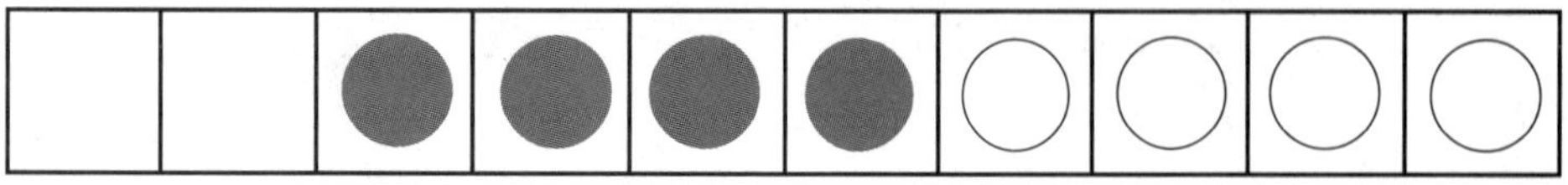

TWO-DIMENSIONAL SHAPES

Unit 3

Lines
Constructing
Circles, Triangles,
Quadrilaterals

Objectives

- identify and describe horizontal and vertical lines
- describe and construct patterns
- use lines in pattern making
- use a compass
- use geometric tools to interpret and meet specifications
- construct and interpret patterns
- select appropriate technology
- construct polygons and other two-dimensional shapes
- meet specifications requiring accurate constructions
- extend a mathematical investigation by asking questions

Language

horizontal, vertical, parallel, sloping, curved, compass, radius, diameter, circle, semicircle, patterns, triangle, protractor, quadrilateral, kite, trapezium, parallelogram

Materials/Resources

paper, compasses, protractors, colored pencils/ felt pens, string, weights, marbles, pens, small pencils, paper, rulers

Contents of Student Pages

* Materials needed for each reproducible student page

Page 47 Lines
horizontal; vertical, sloping; parallel; pattern making

* paper, colored pencils/pens, string, weights, marbles

Page 48 Circles
using a compass to construct circles given radius or diameter; semicircle

* compasses, paper, small pencils, rulers

Page 49 Drawing Circles
making patterns inside a circle using a compass

* compasses, spare paper, colored pencils/pens

Page 50 Triangles
constructing triangles using compasses, given the length of the three sides

* compasses, spare paper

Page 51 Drawing Triangles
constructing triangles using a protractor when given the length of two sides and the included angle, or two angles and one side

* protractors, spare paper, rulers

Page 52 Drawing Quadrilaterals
drawing quadrilaterals using protractors and parallel lines

* compasses, protractors, rulers

Page 53 Assessment
* compasses, protractors, rulers

Remember

Before starting, ensure that each student:
- ❏ is able to use a compass properly, holding it by the top, not the arms
- ❏ has a small pencil to use in a compass

(45)

Additional Activities

- ❏ Have students search in magazines, newspapers, etc., for patterns involving different types of lines. Make a class poster of their findings.
- ❏ Repeat the above using circular designs.
- ❏ Have students construct logos using precise measurement and geometric tools.
- ❏ Students can make a class flat using only vertical lines (or only circles/triangles).
- ❏ Have students write a series of directions for designing a logo.
- ❏ Students can work out how to construct a large circle/triangle in the playground. Provide a variety of materials from which they can choose.
- ❏ Have students draw the Olympic five-ring emblem.

Answers

Page 47 Lines

1. a. H
   b. S
   c. V
   d. S
   e. H
   f. S
   g. V
2. Check individual work.
3. Check individual work.
4. Check individual work.
5. Check individual work.

Page 48 Circles

Check individual work.

Page 49 Drawing Circles

Check individual work.

Page 50 Triangles

1,2. Check individual work.
   3. a. It can vary in length.
      b. More information is needed to give an exact measurement.
   4. a. A triangle cannot be made.
      b. The sum of the length of the two shorter sides must be greater than the length of the third side to make a triangle.

Page 51 Drawing Triangles

1. a. 3 cm
   b. 12.7 cm
2. a. 56 cm 6.8 cm
   b. 8.5 cm 11.2 cm

Page 52 Drawing Quadrilaterals

Check individual work.

Page 53 Assessment

Check individual work.

Name	**Date**

For this activity, you will need string, a heavy weight, a marble, paper, and colored pencils or pens.

Horizontal Lines are lines which are parallel to the horizon.

Vertical Lines are at right angles to horizontal lines. Vertical surfaces are in an upright position.

Parallel Lines are straight lines which will never meet, no matter how far you draw them.

---

1. Under each line, write whether it is horizontal (H), vertical (V), or sloping (S).

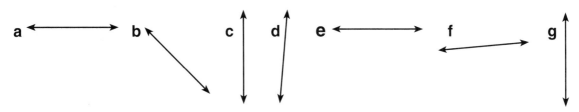

2. Make a plumb line using the string and a heavy weight. Working with a partner, find five surfaces in the classroom which are vertical.

   a. _____   c. _____   e. _____

   b. _____   d. _____

3. Find five horizontal surfaces in the classroom.

   a. _____   c. _____   e. _____

   b. _____   d. _____

4. Here are some interesting line patterns. They use a mixture of types of lines.

   On a piece of paper, draw patterns using:

   a. only vertical and sloping lines   **c.** only curved lines

   b. only sloping lines   **d.** all types of lines

5. Draw a picture of a house in which none of the lines are parallel. Write a sentence about your finished picture.

(47)

Name	**Date**

Work with a partner in this activity.

You will need a compass, a small pencil, and a piece of paper. Remember, when using a compass, hold it at the top, not by the arms.

To draw a circle when you know its radius:

- Use your ruler to set the radius.

- Hold the point of the compass steady on the page.

- Turn the compass steadily, holding it by the top.
  Hint: Mark the center with a small pencil dot so that if
  your compass slips, you can easily find the center.

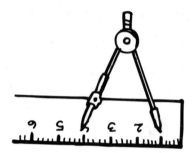

---

1. Draw a circle with a radius of:

    a. 3 cm   **b.** $4\frac{1}{2}$ cm

To draw a circle when you know its diameter:

- Work out the radius by dividing the diameter in half. For example, if the diameter is 8 cm, the radius will be 4 cm.

---

2. On paper draw a semicircle with:

    a. a diameter of 11 cm.   **b.** a radius of 3.8 cm.

48

Name	**Date**

You will need a compass, paper, and colored pencils or felt pens for this activity. Many interesting patterns can be made using a compass. Here is a simple one for you to try.

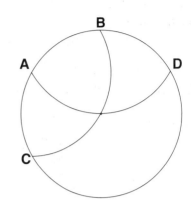

- Draw a circle.

- Mark any point on the circumference (A).

- Be careful not to change the radius on the compass.

- Place the compass point at A and draw the arc which touches the circumference at B and C.

- Now place the compass point at B and draw another arc. It will touch at D and A.

- Place the compass point at D.

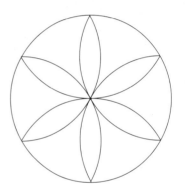

- Continue until your pattern looks like this.

Here are some more patterns you could try. Create two of your own. Color one to make it really attractive.

 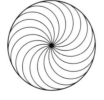  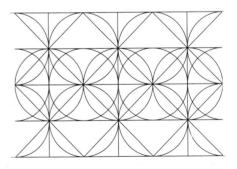

#8999 Targeting Math: Geometry, Chance, and Data

Name	Date

For this activity, you will need a compass and a sharp pencil.

Drawing Triangles

Here's how to draw a triangle with specific measurements.

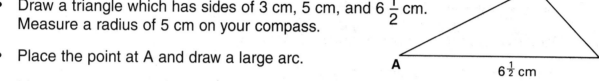

- Draw a triangle which has sides of 3 cm, 5 cm, and $6\frac{1}{2}$ cm. Measure a radius of 5 cm on your compass.

- Place the point at A and draw a large arc.

- Measure a length of 3 cm on your compass. Put the point at B and cut the first arc at C. Join AC and BC.

---

1. In the space below, construct a triangle with sides of $5\frac{1}{2}$ cm, 2 cm, and $4\frac{1}{2}$ cm.

2. On a separate piece of paper, draw these triangles:

   a. sides of 5.2 cm, 4.8 cm, 6 cm

   b. sides of 2.7 cm, 7 cm, 5.5 cm

3. On a separate piece of paper, draw a triangle which has one side of 9 cm and another side of 4 cm.

   a. How long is the third side? _____

   b. Give a brief statement about your answer. _____

4. Draw a triangle of sides 8 cm, 4 cm, and 3 cm.

   a. What happened? _____

   b. Why? _____

50

Name	**Date**

You will need a protractor and spare paper for this activity.

The angle between two sides is called the **included angle**. Here's how to construct a triangle which has sides of 5 cm and $6\frac{1}{2}$ cm and an included angle of 50°.

1. Use your ruler to draw a line AB, which is $6\frac{1}{2}$ cm.

2. With your protractor, draw an angle of 50° at A.

3. Mark a point (C) 5 cm along the new line.

4. Join BC.

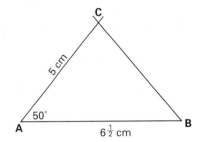

---

1. Draw these triangles on a separate piece of paper.

   a. sides of 5 cm and $3\frac{1}{2}$ cm and an included angle of 38°.

   How long is the third side?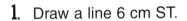

   b. sides of 8 cm and 6.3 cm and an included angle of 125°.

   How long is the third side? _____

Here's how to construct a triangle which has a side of 6 cm and angles at each end of 30° and 72°.

1. Draw a line 6 cm ST.

2. At S draw an angle of 72°.

3. At T draw an angle of 30°.

4. Draw the lines until they meet at W.

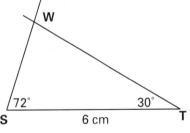

---

2. On a separate piece of paper, draw these triangles.

   a. one side of $7\frac{1}{2}$ cm and the angles at the ends of 60° and 50°.

   b. two angles of 45° and 110° and the side between them is 5 cm. Measure the other two sides in each triangle.

   What are the lengths of the sides?

   a. _____   b. _____

51

Name   **Date**

You will need a compass and a protractor for this activity.

Remember, you can use the edges of a ruler to draw parallel lines.
Here's how to draw a square or rectangle.
Use a protractor to draw the right angles.

- Draw a line of 2.5 cm (AB).

- At A and B make right angles.

- Make two new lines of 2.5 cm (C and D).

- Join C and D.

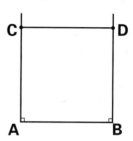

---

1.   Draw a rectangle of sides 4 cm and 2.8 cm.

3.   Draw a kite which has sides of 2 cm and 3.2 cm.
Plan your work before you start.

2.   Copy this trapezoid.

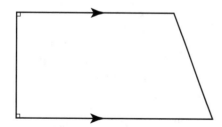

4.   Draw a parallelogram which has sides of 3 cm and 4 cm.
One included angle is 45°.

Name	**Date**

You will need a compass, protractor, and ruler for this page.

1. Look around the room and name:
   a. a horizontal plane.

   b. a vertical plane.

   c. a pair of parallel lines.

2. Construct a triangle which has sides of 3 cm, 4.2 cm and 6 cm.

3. Construct a triangle which has two sides of 3.5 cm and 5 cm and an included angle of 45°.

4. Draw a square with sides of 3 cm.

5. Draw a trapezoid where the parallel sides are 4 cm and 6.5 cm.

6. On a separate piece of paper, construct a circle with a diameter of 10 cm. Using your compass and a ruler, make an interesting pattern in this circle.

(53)

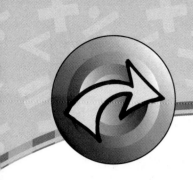

TRANSFORMATION

There is one unit for this topic.

Students learn about transformation by flipping, sliding, and turning shapes. They identify tessellating shapes and make patterns using these shapes.

Students change the size of a shape through scale drawing, and practice exploring shadows and rotational symmetry. They transform shapes by folding.

There is one assessment page.

#8999 Targeting Math: Geometry, Chance, and Data

TRANSFORMATION

Unit 1

Flip
Slide
Turn
Tessellations
Scale Drawing
Symmetry
Shadows

Objectives

- describe, construct, and interpret patterns and tessellations
- recognize that objects can be represented using scale models and make simple calculations using scale
- identify shapes with line symmetry
- describe, construct, and interpret patterns.
- construct and classify polygons and other two-dimensional shapes and describe and compare their patterns
- recognize, visualize, describe, make, and represent three-dimensional objects

Language

design, enlarge, flips, folding, grid, line symmetry, lunar eclipse, origami, patterns, reduce, repeat, rotational symmetry, scales, drawings, shadows, shapes, slides, solar eclipse, solids, tessellations, three-dimensional, turns, unfolded figures, unit of measurement, zenith

Materials/Resources

writing/drawing materials, magazines, computer, newspapers, reference books, glue, rulers, scissors, protractors, rubber bands, cardboard, square- and rectangular-shaped paper, origami books, colored pencils, geoboard

Contents of Student Pages

* Materials needed for each reproducible student page

Remember

Before starting, ensure that you:

❑ relate classroom activities to transformation whenever possible

❑ stress that accuracy is most important in this topic

❑ use a variety of vocabulary when discussing transformation

(55)

Additional Activities

❑ *Investigate Islamic art and architecture for tessellations and patterning. Have students create art designs.*

❑ *Students can construct three-dimensional paper-ring puzzles.*

❑ *Have students practice folding clothes correctly.*

❑ *Have students use computer software such as Microsoft® Word™, Microsoft Publisher™, or a graphics program. to do scale enlargements or reductions,*

❑ *Students can investigate shadows when the sun rises or sets.*

Answers

Page 57 Flips, Slides, and Turns
1. Check individual work.
2. a. slide
   b. flip
   c. turn
3. Check individual work.
4. Check individual work.

Page 58 Patterns and Tesselations
Check individual work.

Page 59 Scale Drawings
1. Check individual work.
2. a. approx. 4 m
   b. cm
   c. 8 m or 800 cm
   d. 10 m or 1,000 cm
   e. 2 m or 200 cm
3. Check individual work.
4. Check individual work.
5. Check individual work.

Page 60 Rotational Symmetry
Check individual work.

Page 61 Shadows
1. Check individual work.
2. a. Virtually none as he is on top of it.
   b. midday
   c. Check individual work.
   d. Check individual work.
   e. the lower the sun, the longer the shadow
3. a. no
   b. full shadow as moon covers sun
   c. complete shadow as sun covers moon
4. a. shadow gets smaller
   b. dark due to total shadow
   c. gets smaller
5. they disappear

Page 62 Folding Shapes
1. Check individual work.
2. a. rectangle
   b. square
   c. Check individual work.
   d. rectangle
   e. Check individual work.
3. Check individual work.
4. Circle answer "b."
5. Check individual work.

Page 63 Assessment
1. Check individual work.
2. Check individual work.
3. Check individual work.
4. Circle answer "b"
5. Check individual work.
6. Check individual work.
7. Check individual work.

56

Name	**Date**

1. Use flips, slides, and turns to continue the patterns.

a. flips **b.** slides **c.** turns

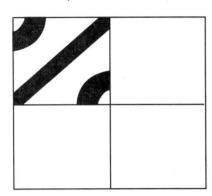 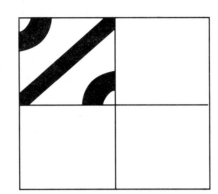 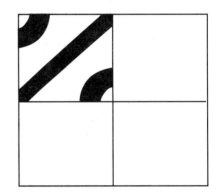

2. Label whether flips, slides, or turns are used. Continue the pattern.

a.  **b.** 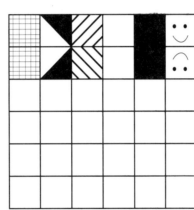 **c.**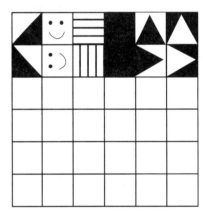

_____ _____ _____

3. Flip, slide, and turn the following shape. Label the new shape.

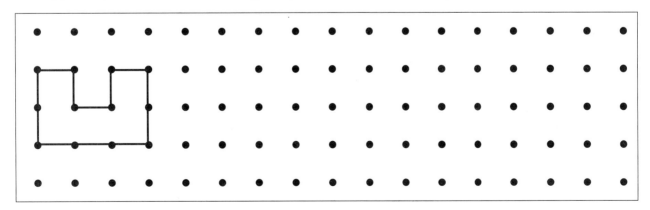

4. On the back of this sheet design your own patterns using flips, slides and turns. Try using solid shapes.

57

Name	**Date**

1. Draw a design in one square. Repeat it to make a pattern.

2. Color these to show tessellating patterns.

   a.   b.   c.

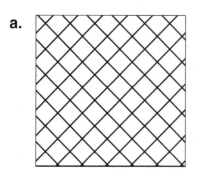 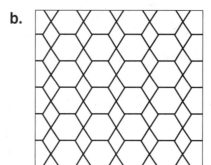 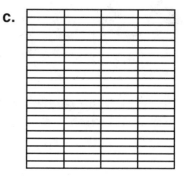

3. Create your own designs using tessellation.

   a.   b.   c.

  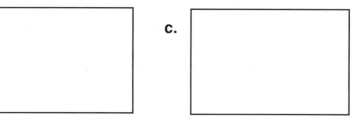

4. Draw two different patterns and tessellations found in the environment. Label what they are and where you found them.

5. Using magazines, newspapers, computer software, copies of reference books, etc., make a collage of pictures where tessellating patterns are used.

58

Name	**Date**

1. Copy these pictures using a 1:1 scale.

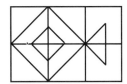  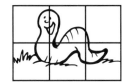 

2. The castle has been drawn to a scale of 1:200.

   a. If the flagpole is 5 meters high, about how high is the door? _____

   b. Which unit of measurement is being used in the scale ratio? _____

   c. How high are the towers? _____

   d. How wide is the castle? _____

   e. Find the width of the windows. _____

3. Enlarge the picture using a 1:2 scale.

 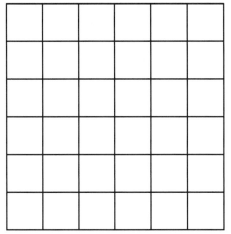

4. Write your initials and then reduce them using a 3:2 scale.

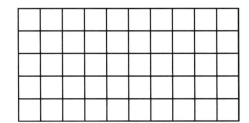 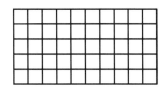

5. On the back of this sheet, glue a picture that you like. Draw a 1 cm grid over it. Enlarge it using a 1:4 scale.

(59)

Name	**Date**

1. List objects that have line symmetry.

_____

_____

2. a. The picture has been made using shapes. Color the shapes which have rotational symmetry. The centers are marked.

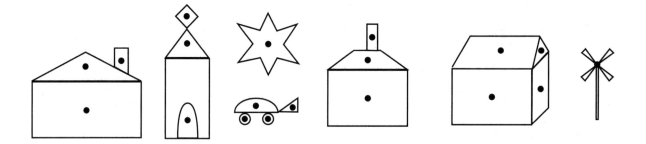

    b. Add to the scene by drawing more pictures which have line symmetry.

3. a. Construct a pattern that has rotational symmetry on a geoboard.

    b. Use that shape to make a cardboard template.

    c. In the space below, trace the template.

    d. Rotate the template around a central point and trace it at different intervals.

    e. Use a protractor to measure the angles. Label them.

4. On the back of this sheet, draw a variety of unusual shapes which have rotational symmetry.

60

Name	**Date**

1. Draw the shadows made by these objects.

   a.    **b.**    **c.**

2. Use the picture to answer the questions.

   a. John is standing directly beneath the sun.
   Draw the shadow he makes.

   b. What time of the day is it? _____

   c. Draw the shadow made after 3 hours and label it (c).

   d. Draw the shadow made after 5 hours and label it (d).

   e. Why does the position of the shadow change? _____

   _____

3. Use the picture to answer the questions.

   a. Would there be a shadow with a solar eclipse?

   _____

   b. Why?

   _____

   c. What would happen in the case of a lunar eclipse?

   _____

4. Imagine that you shine a torch onto an object which gives a shadow.

   a. What happens to the shadow if you move the object away from the torch?

   _____

   b. What happens if the object covers the torch?

   _____

   c. What happens if you keep the object still and you move the distance of the torch?

   _____

5. What happens to shadows when the sun is at its zenith (highest point)?

   _____

61

Name	**Date**

For this activity, you will need one square and one rectangular piece of paper.

1. Use the back of this page to draw the unfolded figures for these objects.

a.    **b.**    **c.**

2. a. Get a rectangular piece of paper and fold it four times. What shape does it make?

_____

   b. Repeat (a) using a square piece of paper. What shape is made?

_____

   c. Predict what shape is made when you fold the square paper five times.

_____

   d. What was the actual shape made?

_____

   e. What happens if you cut through a corner after you have folded the paper in c?

_____

3. Write a procedural text on how to construct a three-dimensional die using its unfolded figure.

_____

_____

_____

_____

_____

_____

_____

4. On a separate piece of paper, draw some packages with unusual shapes. Draw their unfolded figures.

5. Complete folding techniques used in origami to make different objects such as animals. Construct a scene using these objects. Invent a story about them.

62

Name	**Date**

1. Slide this shape seven spaces to the right.

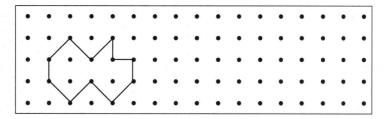

2. Turn this shape 90° clockwise, then flip it. Draw the shape in the new positions.

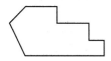

3. Color the shapes which tessellate.

4. Which would be the smaller map of Tasmania? Circle the answer.

   a. 1 cm : 30 km   **b.** 1 cm : 90 km

5. Enlarge this picture using a 1:2 scale.

 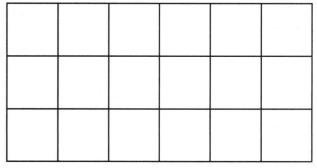

6. Draw the shadows made by these objects.

   a.   **b.**   **c.**

7. On the back of this sheet draw the unfolded figure for:

   a. a die   **b.** an ice-cream cone   **c.** a book

63

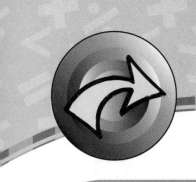

POSITION AND MAPPING

These units use the language of position. Students follow directions, draw paths and maps, and use coordinates to locate specific points. They identify compass points and read maps. They write directions for others to follow.

Students use ordered pairs to plot points in order to draw specific items. They draw lines of longitude and latitude and the equator on a map.

In one activity, false directions sabotage a car rally. In another, teams use coordinates to place four "people" in a row to win a game.

There are two assessment pages.

#8999 Targeting Math: Geometry, Chance, and Data

POSITION AND MAPPING

Unit 1

**Oral Directions
Positional Language
Coordinates
Compass Directions**

Objectives

- use simple coordinates or compass points to mark out points on a grid
- demonstrate a willingness to work cooperatively with others and to value the contributions of others
- appreciate the contribution of mathematics to our society
- give clear instructions for moving and finding objects on plans, using directions
- produce models, labeling key features of a location
- interpret maps
- find paths to satisfy specifications
- describe and label the position of objects in relation to one another
- use mathematical terminology and some conventions to explain, interpret, and represent position

Language

model, direction, draw, map, path, plan, route, row, columns, middle, top, last, grid, maze, location, position, coordinate, plot, compass points

Materials/Resources

paper, scissors, glue, graph paper, equipment for modeling (mathematical and recycled), colored pencils, red and blue pens

Contents of Student Pages

 * *Materials needed for reproducible student page*

. . . .
Remember

Encourage students to:

- ❏ *develop correct use of the language of position and mapping*
- ❏ *assist each other cooperatively*
- ❏ *discuss and visualize their understandings*
- ❏ *work using accuracy and precision*
- ❏ *use rulers when necessary*

(65)

Additional Activities

- ❑ *Have students research their city and its landmarks. Make models, using various sized boxes, etc.*
- ❑ *Have students draw sketches from models.*
- ❑ *"New Word for Today"... expand students' usage of positional Language by using location as often as possible. Reward efforts, e.g., points can be earned toward ½ hour free math time.*
- ❑ *Play directional games, e.g., Ship Shape using terms such as bow (front), stern (back), starboard (right), port (left).*
- ❑ *Have students rearrange class furniture following written directions. They can sketch their ideas for an ideal classroom.*
- ❑ *Using an overhead projector and dot paper, give directions to students to follow a set path.*
- ❑ *Have students use street directories to identify places in relation to your school. For example, Central Park is three blocks north of the school playground.*

Answers

Page 67 Oral Directions

1. Check individual work.

Page 68 Labeling

First row: Ms. Allen, Mr. Stone, Mrs. Watkins, Ms. Boustani

Second row: Miss Stanic, Mr. Hackland, Mrs. Anderson, Mr. Lee

Third row: Mrs. Nichols, Mrs. Game, Miss Bower, Miss McIntyre

Fourth row: Mr. Carpenter, Ms. Auvers, Mr. Singh, Mr. Edwards

Page 69 Road Map

1. Check individual work.
2. Jamie—east along Hope Street
   Rana—south down Mayson Street, west onto Hope Street
   Vance—north along Duck Street, north east along Lumel Street, east along Cohen Road

Page 70 Coordinates

Check individual work.

Page 71 Island Map

Check individual work.

Page 72 Compass Points

1. a. SE
   b. NE
   c. W
   d. E
   e. SW
2. Check individual work.
3. compass

Page 73 Assessment

1. a. NW
   b. SE
   c. S
   d. W
   e. NE
2. 5S, 2E, 2N, 7E, 5SW, 3SE, 3N, 3E, 2S, 1SW, 4W, 1E
3. a. West
   b. North

#8999 Targeting Math: Geometry, Chance, and Data

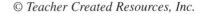

Name	**Date**

For this activity, you will need to work with a partner.

1. Cut and paste the following rooms to create your ideal home.

2. Give your partner directions to create the same home. Do not let your partner look at your plan. He or she needs to simply follow the directions you say.

3. Compare your results. List the advantages and disadvantages of oral directions.

Advantages   **Disadvantages**

_____   _____

_____   _____

_____   _____

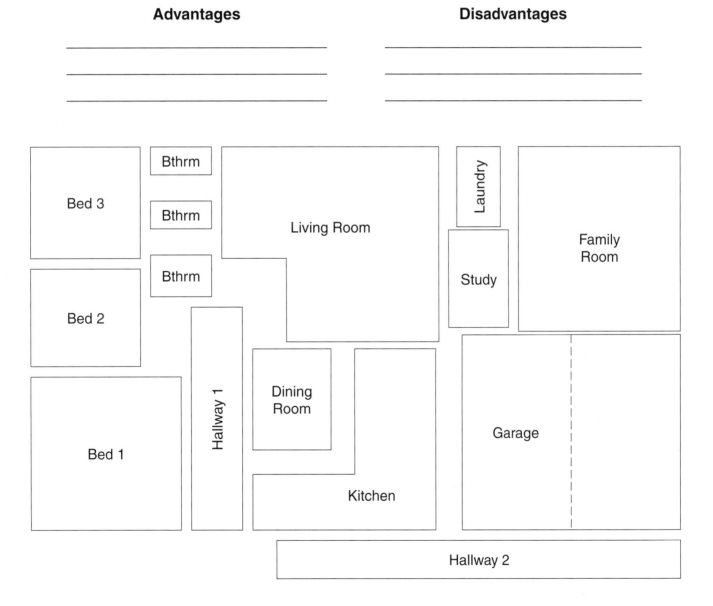

4. Using various classroom resources, design a scene and describe it to your partner. Try adding coordinate instructions, compass directions, or distances to obtain greater accuracy.

67

Name		**Date**	

Label the teacher's mailboxes according to the school secretary's instructions.

Ms. Allen			

1. Ms. Allen—first hole, top row
2. Mrs. Anderson—second row, third hole
3. Ms. Auvers—second column, last hole
4. Miss Bower—new teacher
5. Ms. Boustani—last column, first hole
6. Mr. Carpenter—first column, last hole
7. Mr. Edwards—last hole, bottom row
8. Mrs. Game—above Ms. Auvers
9. Mr. Hackland—between Mrs. Game and Mr. Stone
10. Mr. Lee—next to Mrs. Anderson
11. Miss McIntyre—below Mr. Lee
12. Mrs. Nichols—below Miss Stanic
13. Mr. Singh—left of Mr. Edwards
14. Miss Stanic—first column
15. Mr. Stone—right of Ms. Allen
16. Mrs. Watkins—third column, first hole

Extension Activity

Design your own instructions to label mailboxes for teachers at your school. Use words such as "diagonally opposite," "above," "below," "between," etc.

68

Name

Date

Locate these children's homes on the map.

1. Jamie
3. Rana
5. Vance
7. Selina

2. Ira
4. Ben
6. Stewart
8. Zoe

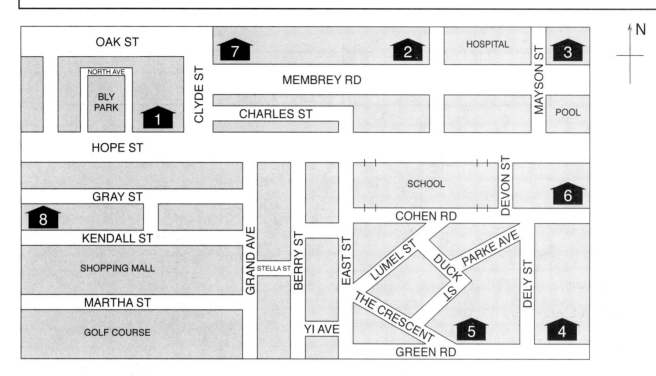

1. On a separate piece of paper, write directions to help the children reach their destinations.

2. Record the shortest route for Jamie to school. Repeat this for Rana and Vance. Compare your answers with a partner's.

69

Name	**Date**

Remember

When locating coordinate points, read across ←——→ , then up or down ↕ .

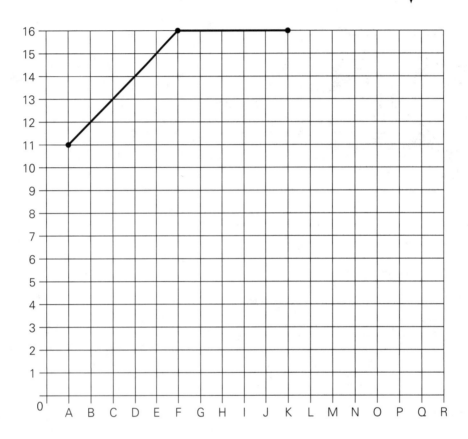

Using a ruler:

Connect (K, 16) (F,16) (A,11) (A,6) (F,1) (K,1) (P,6) (P,11) (K,16)

Connect (A,11) (P,11)   Connect (A,6) (P,6)   Connect (F,1) (F,16)   Connect (K,1) (K,16)

Connect (H,16) (H,13)   Connect (I,16) (I,13)   Connect (H,4) (H,1)   Connect (I,4) (I,1)

Connect (A,9) (D,9)   Connect (A,8) (D,8)   Connect (M,9) (P,9)   Connect (M,8) (P,8)

Connect (D,13) (M,4)   Connect (D,4) (M,13)   Connect (D,4) (M,4)   Connect (M,13) (D,13)

Color in your design.

Extension Activity

Create a maze using graph paper. Compile all the mazes into an Amazing Mazes Workbook.

Name	**Date**

Children's Island

Follow the directions to locate the cities.

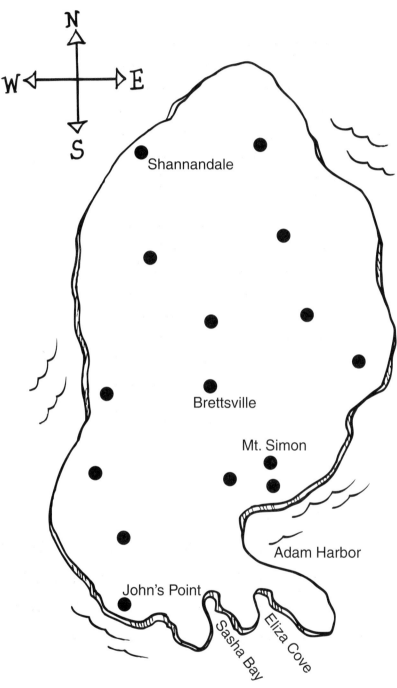

Margaretside—W of Brettsville

Peterwood—E of Lynfields

Clareville—N of Brettsville

Theo Hills—E of Shannandale

Garycastle—S of Margaretside

Conbury—S of Mt. Simon

Robhurst—NW of Adam Harbor

Marylands—E of Brettsville

Lynfields—S of Shannandale

Jessicatown—N of John's Point

Gail Grove—E of Clareville

Research

Working together in small groups, research your nearest capital city. Select and list five to ten landmarks using maps and street directories. Compare landmarks in relation to one another. Construct a model depicting these landmarks. Report your findings to the class.

71

Name

Date

1. Identify the compass direction indicated.

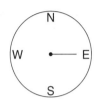

a. _____   **b.** _____   **c.** _____   **d.** _____   **e.** _____

2. Label the compass as shown. Take care to observe where North is located.

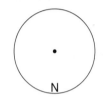
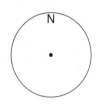

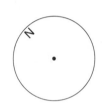

a. West   **b.** South   **c.** North East   **d.** South West   **e.** North West

3. Follow the path. . . 4 paces East (already marked), 5 South, 3 West, 2 South, 5 East, 6 North, 10 E, 6 SW, 2 S, 4 NE, 5 E, 1 N, 5 W, 3 SE, 1 E.

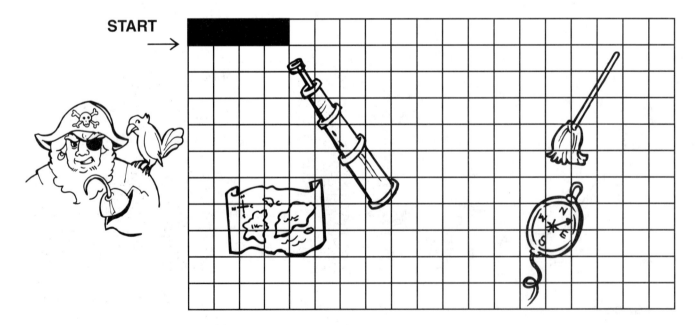

What piece of equipment has the pirate forgotten? _____

#8999 Targeting Math: Geometry, Chance, and Data

Name	**Date**

1. Identify the compass direction indicated.

a.  **b.**  **c.**  **d.** 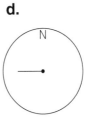 **e.**

SE	W	NW	S	NE

2. Give directions for the camera man to find his television crew.

5 paces south,_____

_____

_____

_____

_____

_____

_____

3. If Vanessa walked 8 miles north, then 8 miles east, what direction is

    a. behind her? _____   **b.** on her left? _____

73

Name	Date

Four Points in a Row

Materials: one piece of graph paper for each game, a red pen and a blue pen

Number of players: two teams of two players

Aim: To get four points in a row vertically, horizontally, or diagonally.

How to play: Draw a grid up to 10 x 10 on the graph paper. Teams take turns calling out an ordered pair. They then color that point. Play continues until one team has claimed four points in a row.

Rules: Coordinates cannot be changed once they have been stated. If a point has already been marked the pair misses a turn.

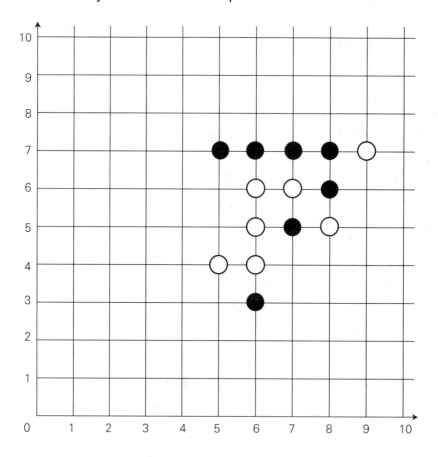

Variations: Get five points in a row. Play with three or four teams.

POSITION AND MAPPING

Unit 2

Oral Directions
Coordinates
Compass Directions
Longitude and Latitude

Objectives

- *use simple coordinates to describe position and mark out points on a grid*
- *give unambiguous instructions for moving and finding objects on maps and plans, using directions and compass points*
- *interpret maps*
- *find paths to satisfy specifications*
- *describe and label the position of objects in relation to one another*
- *use mathematical terminology and some conventions to explain, interpret, and represent mathematical situations*

Language

positional words, model, direction, draw, map, path, plan, route, row, columns, middle, top, last, grid, maze, location, position, coordinate, plot, compass, compares, points, north, south, east, west, north-east, south-east, north-west, south-west

Materials/Resources

globe, atlas, dictionary

Contents of Student Pages

* *Materials needed for each reproducible student page*

Page 77 Coded Message
  reading a message using coordinate points

Page 78 Symmetrical Coordinates
  plotting coordinates; adding lines of symmetry; designing own symmetrical picture

Page 79 Car Rally
  identifying missing compass directions

Page 80 Longitude and Latitude
  understanding and plotting the lines of longitude and latitude

  * *atlas, globe*

Page 81 Assessment

Remember

Encourage students to:
  - ❏ *develop correct use of the language of position and mapping*
  - ❏ *use the school grounds for activities*
  - ❏ *develop their own positional activities*
  - ❏ *explore positioning, sailing, and navigation*
  - ❏ *use various maps*
  - ❏ *work accurately and precisely*

(75)

Additional Activities

- ❑ Allow students to play computer chess using coordinate points to move pieces.
- ❑ Have students set out an orienteering event in the playground, local park, etc.
- ❑ Students can design a self-guided tour map of the school for visitors.
- ❑ Have students use a street directory to plan a journey/excursion.
- ❑ Have students walk through a maze set up in the classroom.
- ❑ Students can observe a world map and locate the position of countries in relation to each other, for example: New Zealand is south-east of Australia.
- ❑ Invite guest speakers to explain how directions are used in their occupations, such as a pilot, ambulance officer, or a ship's captain.
- ❑ Students can use street directions to identify places in relation to your school. For example, Central Park is three blocks north of the school playground.

Answers

Page 77 Coded Message
"Prepare a message to your friend using the alphabetical coordinate grid."

Page 78 Symmetrical Coordinates
1.–2. Check individual work.

Page 79 Car Rally
1. c

Page 80 Longitude and Latitude
1. Latitude—distance east and west
   Longitude—distance north and south
2–4. Check individual work.

Page 81 Assessment
1. Check individual work.
2. a. False
   b. True
3–4. Check individual work.

#8999 Targeting Math: Geometry, Chance, and Data

Name   **Date**

Use the coordinates to decipher the coded message.

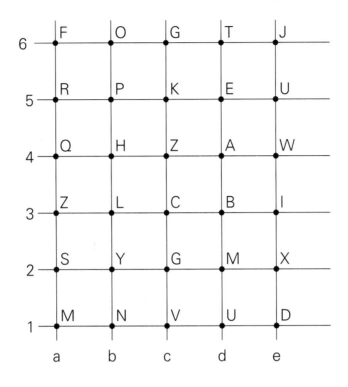

___ ___ ___ ___ ___ ___ ___   ___   ___ ___ ___ ___ ___ ___ ___
(b,5) (a,5) (d,5) (b,5) (d,4) (a,5) (d,5)   (d,4)   (d,2) (d,5) (a,2) (a,2) (d,4) (c,2) (d,5)

___ ___   ___ ___ ___ ___   ___ ___ ___ ___ ___ ___
(d,6) (b,6)   (b,2) (b,6) (e,5) (a,5)   (a,6) (a,5) (e,3) (d,5) (b,1) (e,1)

___ ___ ___ ___ ___   ___ ___ ___
(e,5) (a,2) (e,3) (b,1) (c,2)   (d,6) (b,4) (d,5)

___ ___ ___ ___ ___ ___ ___ ___ ___ ___ ___ ___
(d,4) (b,3) (b,5) (b,4) (d,4) (d,3) (d,5) (d,6) (e,3) (c,3) (d,4) (b,3)

___ ___ ___ ___ ___ ___ ___ ___ ___ ___   ___ ___ ___ ___.
(c,3) (b,6) (b,6) (a,5) (e,1) (e,3) (b,1) (d,4) (d,6) (d,5)   (c,2) (a,5) (e,3) (e,1)

#8999 Targeting Math: Geometry, Chance, and Data

Name   **Date**

1. Plot the coordinates as directed. Draw a line to show symmetry.

a.

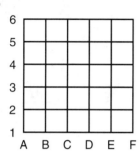

D1, B1, A2, A3, B4,
D4, E3, E2, D1

b.

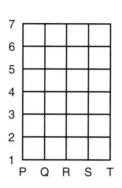

P2, R2, T3, T6,
R7, P7, P2

c.

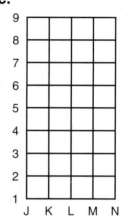

K8, K7, J7, J6, K6, K5,
J5, J4, K4, K3, J3, J2,
K2, K1, N1, N2, M2, M3,
N3, N4, M4, M5, N5, N6,
M6, M7, N7, N8, K8

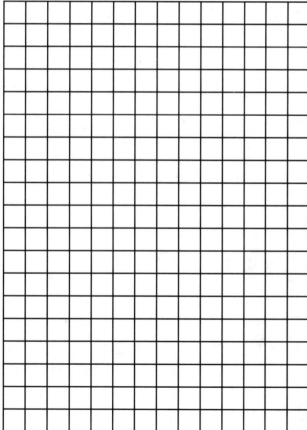

2. **a.** Design your own symmetrical picture.

   b. Add the axis of symmetry line.

   c. Plot your design.

   d. Mark in the x axis and the y axis.

   e. Record the coordinate points.

   _____

   _____

   _____

   _____

   _____

   _____

78

Name   **Date**

The Car Rally has been sabotaged! Choose the correct piece to put back into the directions to lead the competitors safely across the uncharted lands.

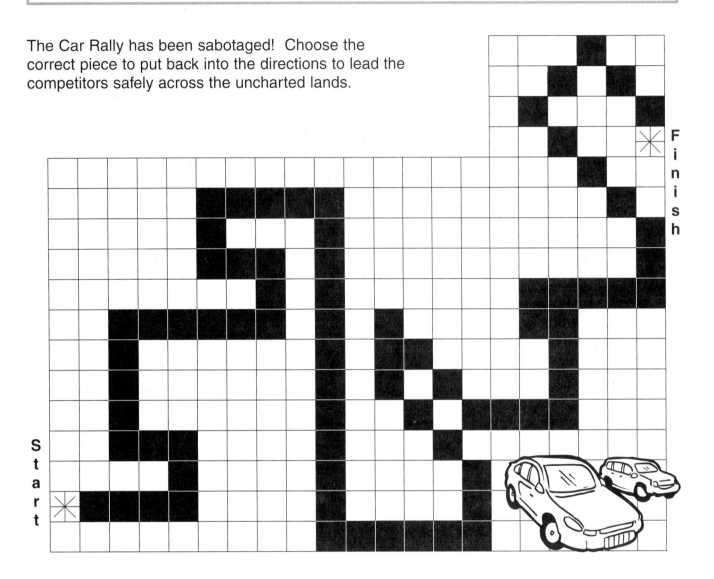

ANNUAL CAR RALLY DIRECTIONS
START 4E, 2N,   2N,
2W,   5E, 2N, 3NW,
2N, 3SE, 3E,   1N, 4E, 2N,
4NW, 2   FINISH

a.   2W, 4N, 3E,
2N, 4E, 10S,
     2N, 4W,
      NW, 2S

b.   2W, 4N, 5E,
2N, 4W, 11S,
     3N, 1E,
      NW, 2E

c.   2W, 4N, 5E,
2N, 4E, 11S,
     3N, 1W,
      NE, 2SE

(79)

Name	**Date**

Research

1. What are lines of latitude and longitude?

   _____

   _____

2. Who would use these lines and why?

   _____

   _____

3. **a.** Using an atlas, draw a map of the United States.

   b. Plot in lines of latitude and longitude.

4. These lines are north of the Equator. Locate, on a globe, the corresponding lines of latitude and longitude in the Southern Hemisphere. Name some countries they pass through.

   _____

   _____

Name	**Date**

1. Draw a line from the center to the correct compass point for each of the compasses below.

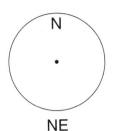 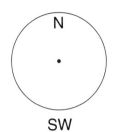 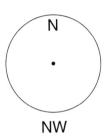 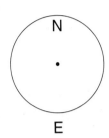 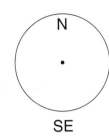

NE   SW   NW   E   SE

2. True or False

    a. Lines of latitude run north to south. _____

    b. NNW lies between north and north west. _____

3. Draw a scene.

4. Write five positional phrases to describe your scene.

    a. _____

    b. _____

    c. _____

    d. _____

    e. _____

81

CHANCE AND DATA

These two units explore the concept of an event being possible, impossible, likely, unlikely, or certain.

Students practice the skills of collecting, recording, representing and organizing data. They draw and interpret graphs and learn to graphically represent data in more than one way.

Students make and check predictions. They toss coins and spin spinners to predict outcomes, and study TV viewing patterns and programs to predict good times for certain advertisements. They interpret graphs to learn from collected data.

Also discussed in these units are mean, median, and mode and their uses. Students use their names in an exercise to explore these measures and make inferences.

Racing elephants help students work out the chances of correctly predicting results on the activity page.

There are two assessment pages.

#8999 Targeting Math: Geometry, Chance, and Data

CHANCE AND DATA

Unit 1

Graphs
Data
Notation
Terminology
Predictions
Interpretation

Objectives

- *interpret data*
- *display, read, and interpret a variety of graphs*
- *compare different representations of the same data*
- *recognize the economy and power of mathematical notation, terminology and convention in helping to develop and communicate mathematical ideas*
- *represent, interpret, and explain mathematical situations using everyday Language with some mathematical terminology, including simple graphs and diagrams*
- *pose questions and collect data*
- *contribute to discussions to clarify which data would help answer particular questions or test predictions, and take care in collecting data*
- *appreciate the impact of mathematical information on daily life*
- *record and identify all possible outcomes arising from chance experiments*
- *comment on predictions made in light of the results of data collected*
- *become involved in a physical experiment to develop intuitive understanding of probability theory*
- *consider predictions after data collections*

Language

mean, mode, median, likely, unlikely, chance, predict, guess, extension, statement, graph, information, survey, representations, abstract, pictorial, data

Materials/Resources

coins, paper, cardboard, calculator, large sheets of paper, ruler, graph paper, coins (a variety), hexagonal pencils, playing cards (a variety), small white stickers, colored pencils

Contents of Student Pages

   * *Materials needed for each reproducible student page*

Page 85 Collecting Data
   tossing coins; using a spinner

   * *coins*

Page 86 Interpreting Graphs
   answering questions; deciding on quality questions

   * *spare paper*

Page 87 Picture Graphs Using Symbols
using symbols and part symbols; both vertical and horizontal graphs

Page 88 Drawing Picture Graphs
using symbols and part symbols; both vertical and horizontal graphs

Page 89 Reading Column Graphs
both vertical and horizontal graphs

Page 90 Drawing Column Graphs
both vertical and horizontal graphs

Page 91 Drawing Line Graphs
using coordinates; answering questions

Page 92 Conversion Graphs
using graphs to convert measurements; completing graphs

Page 93 Drawing Bar Graphs
using percentages and measurement

Page 94 Drawing Pie Graphs
calculating proportions of 360°

   * *calculator, protractor*

Page 95 Survey Graphs
gathering data from survey questions; displaying data using column and pie graphs

   * *calculator, protractor*

Page 96 Types of Graphs
using different types of graphs

   * *scissors, glue*

Page 97 Predictions
predicting results; carrying out experiments

   * *hexagonal pencils, white stickers, spare paper, colored pencils*

Page 98 Experiments
using cards; listing possibilities; testing predictions

   * *playing cards*

Page 99 Mean, Mode, and Median
working out mean, mode, and median using values for letters.

Page 100 Assessment
Page 101 Activity Page
predicting winners

Remember

Before starting, ensure that each student:

- ❏ *understands that graphs are an everyday application of mathematical skills and knowledge*
- ❏ *knows that accuracy is important when measuring distance for bar graphs*
- ❏ *checks answers*
- ❏ *reads problem solving questions twice*

Additional Activities

❑ *Encourage children to justify their answers to peers. The justification process requires an ordering of thoughts and a depth of understanding.*

Answers

Page 85 Collecting Data
1. b. 5:25/1:5
   c. 10:25/2:5
   d. 6:25
   e. 1:25
2. three
   one
   two
   four
   five
3. Check individual work.

Page 86 Interpreting Graphs
1. no, yes, no, yes, yes, yes
2. Check individual work.

Page 87 Picture Graphs Using Symbols
1. a. 1999
   b. 2001
   c. 75
   d. 3 years
2. a. June
   b. March
   c. 3 months
   d. (iii)
   e. $950
3. Check individual work   f. Check individual work.

Page 88 Drawing Picture Graphs
1. Check individual work.
2. Pop 4
   Rock 5
   Classic 7
   Country 3
3. Check individual work.

Page 89 Reading Column Graphs
1. a. False
   b. False
   c. False
   Circle e.
2. a. City
   b. Check individual work.
   c. No
   d. 115
   e. 25
   f. 1 square = 5 families
   g. True

Page 90 Drawing Column Graphs
1. a.–d. Check individual work.
   e. 255 lbs.
2. Check individual work.
   a. 5 squares = 100 tickets or 1 square = 20 tickets
   b. Gymnastics, Hockey
   c. No
   d. (circle iv)

Page 91 Drawing Line Graphs
1. a. iii 4:00 P.M.
   b. 1 P.M.–2 P.M.
      3 P.M.–4 P.M.
   c. ii
2. a. Check individual work.
   b. 32°
   c. 30°
   d. 4 P.M.

Page 92 Conversion Graphs
1. a. 16 km   c. 80 km
   b. 25 m   d. True
2. a. Check individual work.
   b. 750 mL
   c. 5 cups
   d. 625 mL
   e. 300 mL

Page 93 Drawing Bar Graphs
Check individual work.

Page 94 Drawing Pie Graphs
1. 60°, 120°, 90°, 60°, 30°

Page 95 Survey Graphs
Check individual work.

Page 96 Types of Graphs
1. Check individual work.
2. Pie chart—One third of our family likes chocolate ice-cream.
   Line graph—The weight of one person over seven years.
   Column graph—There are six boys in our class.
   Picture graph—Eye color
   Venn diagram—Girls and boys who wear red sweaters to school.

Page 97 Predictions
1. In general: there is a one in two chance.
2. In general: there is a one in three chance.
3. In general: there is a one in six chance.
4. Spinner 1
   Spinner 2
   Spinner 1

Page 98 Experiments
1. Actual 6
2. Actual 24
3. Actual 24, 12
4. Actual 4, True

Page 99 Mean, Median, and Mode
Check individual work.

Page 100 Assessment
1. a. True
   b. False
   c. False
   d. True
2.–3. Check individual work.

Page 101 Activity Page
1. a.–d In general, ½

   b. $\frac{1}{16}$, 16, 16
2. a.– e. Check individual work.
   f. $\frac{1}{32}$; 32; 32
3–4. Check individual work.

84

Name	**Date**

1. Using the grid below, what is the chance of tossing a coin and having it land on:

   a. a number two square?

   Answer: There are three number two squares out of 25 squares so there are three chances out of 25.

   b. a number one square?_____

   c. a number three square? _____

   d. a number five square?_____

   e. a number four square? _____

1	2	3	3	1
3	3	5	5	3
4	3	1	2	3
5	5	5	5	3
1	3	2	3	1

2. Using a spinning wheel like the one below, what is the order of patterns that the wheel would most likely land on?

   _____

   _____

   _____

   _____

   _____

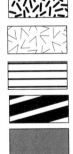

3. Make a spinner of your own that gives:
   - one chance in eight of landing on red
   - two chances in eight of landing on green
   - three chances in eight of landing on blue
   - two chances in eight of landing on yellow

When you have finished, try your spinner.

Predict the amount of times it will land on each color after 40 spins.

Keeping a record of spins and outcomes, spin the spinner 40 times.

Use the information (data) you collected to make a statement of what happened.

85

Name	Date

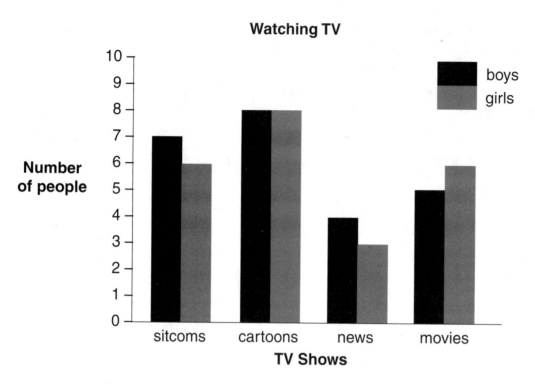

1. It is important to think about the information in a graph. Could the following questions be answered from the information given in the graph above?

   a. What is the best time to advertise a new game for boys?_____

   b. Is there is a difference between the programs boys like and girls like? _____

   c. On what station are the favorite programs shown? _____

   d. Are the cartoons the most popular television programs? _____

   e. Do more boys than girls watch the news?_____

   f. Do boys and girls like to watch movies? _____

2. Use a separate piece of paper for this question. Think of your own survey question.

   a. Make a list of 10 people to ask.

   b. Decide how to keep track of the answers.

   c. Decide on the type of graph you will use to present your information.

   d. Prepare a graph and a report on the data you collected.

   e. Present your report and graph to the class. Make a list of other things your results could tell people.

Name	**Date**

Symbols are used for a group of items in picture graphs.

1. a. During which year did the company have least work? _____

b. In which year were 35 houses built?
_____

c. How many houses were built in 2001 and 2002 together? _____

d. How many years did it take to double the 1999 building completions?
_____

Key: ⌂ = 10 houses built   ▯ = 5 houses built

1999	⌂ ⌂
2000	⌂ ⌂ ▯
2001	⌂ ⌂ ⌂ ▯
2002	⌂ ⌂ ⌂ ⌂
2003	⌂ ⌂ ⌂ ⌂ ⌂

Key: $ = $25

Title: _____

(picture graph of $ symbols)

Feb Mar Apr May Jun

2. Fifth grade students published this graph to show their fundraising success.
a. Which month was their best? _____
b. In which month did they raise $200?
_____

c. How many months did they take to raise their first $500? _____

d. This graph could be used to:
  i. plan next year's fundraising.
  ii. show the principal their efforts.
  iii. show the best fundraiser in the year.
  iv. show how the money was spent.

e. How much short of their $2,000 target are the fifth grade students? _____

f. Give the graph a title.

3. Draw suitable symbols and numbers that could be used for these graphs.

a. Books borrowed from the Alexander Library _____ = _____ books

b. Plane departures on Christmas Eve. _____ = _____ departures

c. Dog licenses issued by the Council _____ = _____ licenses

#8999 Targeting Math: Geometry, Chance, and Data

Name	**Date**

1. **a.** Using the symbol ▯ = 10 cans collected, complete the picture graph to show the information listed below.

Danny collected 80 cans.

Sean collected 95 cans.

Mike collected 75 cans.

Freddy collected 85 cans.

Ray collected 65 cans.

Danny	
Sean	
Mike	
Freddy	
Ray	

   b. Give the graph a title.

2. Two graphs were prepared by two groups of children to show the same results of a survey on types of concerts attended by families in the last year. Complete the second graph.

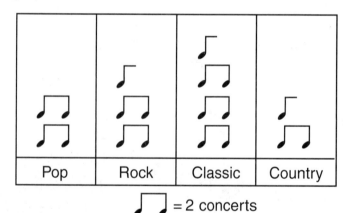

	Pop	Rock	Classic	Country

♪♪ = 2 concerts

Pop	
Rock	
Classic	
Country	

⊙ = 1 concert

3. Transfer the information below to the picture graph. Decide on the scale.

Hits made in softball games, summer 2001

Jan   卌 卌 卌 ||

Jenny 卌 卌 卌 卌

Fiona 卌 卌 |||

Tiu   卌 卌 卌 卌

Jenny	Jenny	Fiona	Tiu

⊗ = _____ hits

Name	**Date**

1. This graph shows the number of minutes of exercise done by Jason in a week.

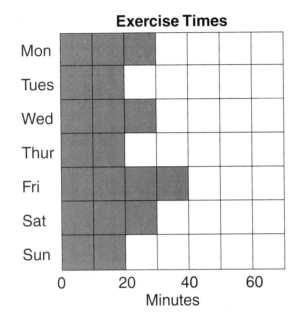

Answer True or False to these questions.

a. Jason does more exercise in one weekend session than on any weekday.

b. Exercise time on Fri and Sat combined is more than on Sun, Mon, Tues.

c. The exercise time increases evenly.

Circle the letter(s) that show the information which can be found on this graph.

d. Who does the exercise?

e. Exercise days and times.

f. Exercise is good for you.

g. 85 minutes of exercise is done on the weekend.

2. This graph shows the holiday destinations chosen by families from Hudatwerk.

a. Which destination is least popular? _____

b. Which holiday would you choose?_____

c. If 15 more families had chosen Overseas would they equal Mountains?_____

d. How many families were surveyed?_____

e. How many more families chose Beach than chose Country?_____

f. What scale is used on the vertical axis?

1 square = _____ families

g. True or False: This graph shows where some families like to go for vacations. _____

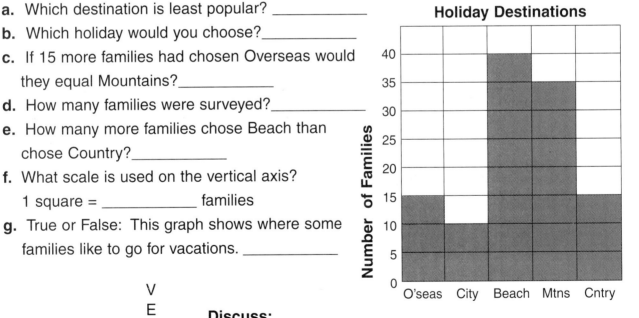

V
E
R
HORIZONTAL
I
C
A
L

Discuss:

What does the horizontal axis show in each graph?

What does the vertical axis show?

Can they be reversed?

#8999 Targeting Math: Geometry, Chance, and Data

Name   **Date**

1. Complete this graph to show:
   a. house number 44–50 lb of garbage
   b. house number 46–15 lb less than number 44
   c. house number 48–5 lb more than number 38
   d. Label the vertical axis.
   e. What is the total weight of garbage for the group?

   _____

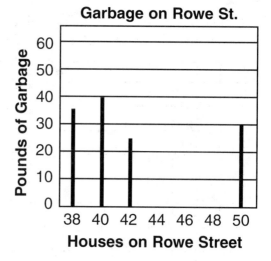

2. Ticket Orders, Olympic Events, Collins High School.
   Complete the graph to show this information. Add these labels to the graph:

   140 Handball, 230 Volleyball, 180 Softball, 290 Gymnastics, 210 Soccer, 280 Hockey

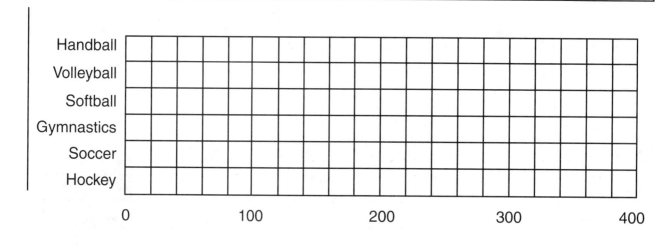

   _____

   a. What scale is used on the horizontal axis? _____

   b. What are the two most popular sports? _____

   c. Mrs. Johns, the school secretary, counted 1,230 ticket orders. Is that the same total that you have? _____

   d. Circle the correct answer.

      This graph shows:

                i. sports played at Collins High.
                ii. tickets allocated for Olympic events.
                iii. spectators at Olympic events.
                iv. tickets ordered for Olympic events.

Name	Date

1. Use the coordinates provided to plot the progress of Jack's car as he drives to Donaville. He left home at 11 A.M. Connect the points to show the progress of the car.

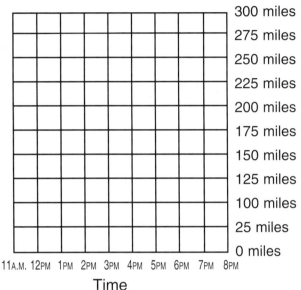

300 miles
275 miles
250 miles
225 miles
200 miles
175 miles
150 miles
125 miles
100 miles
25 miles
0 miles

Distance

11A.M. 12PM 1PM 2PM 3PM 4PM 5PM 6PM 7PM 8PM

Time

1 P.M.—125 miles

2 P.M.—175 miles

3 P.M.—200 miles

4 P.M.—250 miles

5 P.M.—250 miles

6 P.M.—275 miles

   a. When did Jack take a rest from driving?
   i. 1:00 P.M.   ii. 4:00 P.M.   iii. 11 A.M.

   b. During which hours did he cover 50 miles?_____

   c. Circle the information which is not in the graph.
   i.   Jack's speed
   ii. Distance from Evans to Donaville
   iii. Distance traveled in the first six hours of Jack's trip.

2. **a.** Show the **Temperature Variations for Wednesday** on this line graph.

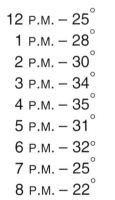

12 P.M. – 25°
1 P.M. – 28°
2 P.M. – 30°
3 P.M. – 34°
4 P.M. – 35°
5 P.M. – 31°
6 P.M. – 32°
7 P.M. – 25°
8 P.M. – 22°

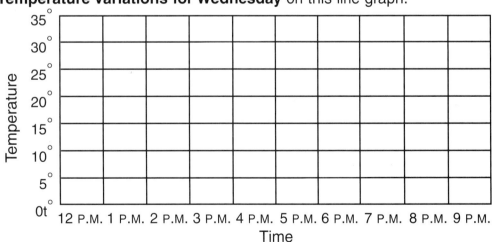

35°
30°
25°
20°
15°
10°
5°
0t

Temperature

12 P.M. 1 P.M. 2 P.M. 3 P.M. 4 P.M. 5 P.M. 6 P.M. 7 P.M. 8 P.M. 9 P.M.

Time

   b. What temperature was it at 6:00 P.M.?_____

   c. What temperature was it at 2:30 P.M.?_____

   d. During which hour was the temperature the highest?_____

⑨1

Name	**Date**

Line graphs can be used to convert measurements. This graph converts miles to kilometers.

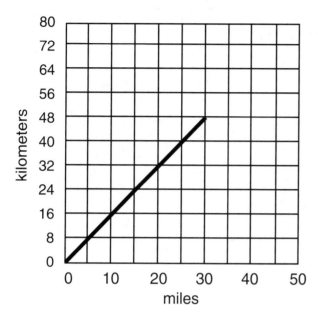

1. **a.** How many kilometers are there in 10 miles?

   _____

   b. How many miles are there in 40 kilometers?

   _____

   c. Continue the line to find how many kilometers there are in 50 miles.

   _____

   d. True or False: A mile is longer than a kilometer.

   _____

2. This graph converts milliliters to cups for measurement of liquids.

   a. 1 cup = 250 mLs. Continue to plot the points for 2 cups, 3 cups, 4 cups, and on to 6 cups.

   b. How many mL are there in 3 cups?

   _____

   c. How many cups are there in 1250 mL?

   _____

   d. How many mL are there in $2\frac{1}{2}$ cups?

   _____

   e. How much more than 2 cups is 800 mL?

   _____

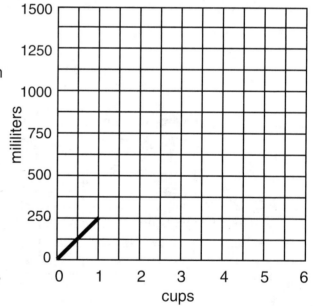

Name	Date

A bar graph represents a whole group as a unit.

To draw a bar graph, we must calculate the size of the whole group, and decide on a length of the bar. If 50 men, 30 women, and 20 children are shown on a bar graph, the bar could be 100 mm long. 1 person = 1 mm. Therefore, 50 men = 50 mm, 30 women = 30 mm, 20 children = 20 mm.

Men	Women	Children

---

1. On the bar graph of 10 cm, show 45 sheep, 10 horses, 35 cattle and 10 pigs on Mr. Jigg's farm. One animal = 1 mm. Label each section.

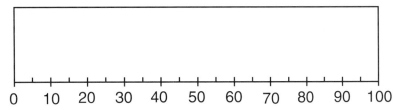

```
   0   10  20  30  40  50  60  70  80  90  100
```

2. On this bar graph, show the amounts of rubbish collected on Clean Up Day as sections of the bar. Label the sections.

   Car parts = 20 tons   Metal = 12 tons
   Plastic = 8 tons   Toys = 5 tons
   Shopping trolleys = 5 tons

3. **a.** Andy has been given $200 for his 13th birthday. He plans to spend 25% of it on CDs, 10% on magazines, 50% on clothes, and the remainder on a concert. Draw the bar graph to represent these amounts.

   b. How much will he have for the concert? _____

#8999 Targeting Math: Geometry, Chance, and Data

Name	Date

To draw pie graphs, divide a circle (360°) into sectors to illustrate the relative proportions of various data. Use a protractor for the angles. For this graph, 100 children were asked what their favorite sports are. 25 chose soccer, 40 chose basketball, 20 chose baseball, and 15 chose tennis.

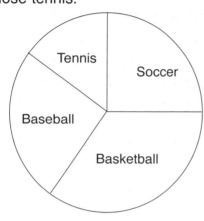

Soccer = $\frac{1}{4}$ of 360° = 90°

Construct a 90° angle at the center.

Basketball = $\frac{2}{5}$ of 360° = 144°

Construct an angle of 144°.

Complete these angles.

Baseball = $\frac{1}{5}$ = 72°

Tennis = $\frac{3}{20}$ = 54°

The main advantage of a pie graph is that it shows comparative data easily and quickly. It is not good for showing small differences in data.

1. Show this data on the pie graph. Use a calculator.

Time spent on a school day		
eating	4 hrs	$\frac{1}{6}$ of 360° = _____ °
sleeping	8 hrs	$\frac{1}{3}$ of 360° = _____ °
school	6 hrs	$\frac{1}{4}$ of 360° = _____ °
playing and homework	4 hrs	$\frac{1}{6}$ of 360° = _____ °
jobs	2 hrs	$\frac{1}{12}$ of 360° = _____ °

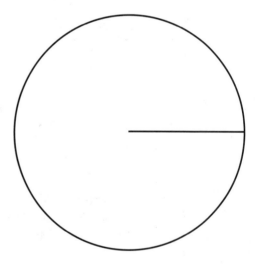

#8999 Targeting Math: Geometry, Chance, and Data   © *Teacher Created Resources, Inc.*

Name	**Date**

Graphs display the data found from an information gathering exercise. Who would use graphs? Marketers, car sales people, local councils, government departments, educators, and anyone else who communicates data to the public. One way to find data about people is to survey them. Questions on the survey are important. They must be clear and obtain the information you are seeking. Discuss suitable questions for surveys.

1. Conduct a survey about choices amongst your class members. Complete the table. Then draw a column graph and a pie graph to show the survey results. Use a calculator to calculate size of sectors in the pie graph.

   a.

Title:	
Choice 1	Choice 4
Choice 2	Choice 5
Choice 3	Other

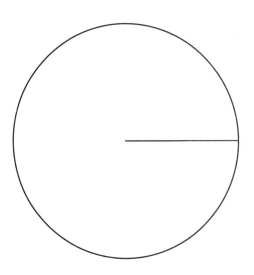

   b. Which graph portrays your data most satisfactorily? Why?

   _____

   _____

   _____

95

Name					Date		

1. Draw lines to match the written questions with the picture answers below.

Three ways to say 10	Model of ratio 3 to 4	Twenty-five percent	One half	two plus five	four team sports final	Speed limit of 60km/h	Three quarters

2. A graph is a picture of information. Cut out and paste together the matching Statement, Type of Graph, and Graph.

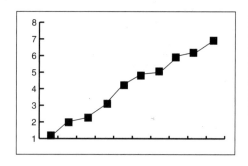

One-third of our family likes chocolate ice-cream.

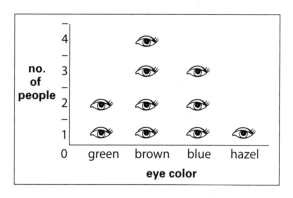

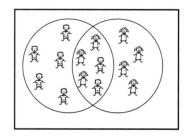

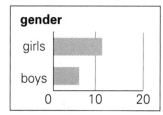

Girls and boys who wear red sweaters to school.

The weight of one person over seven years.

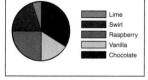

There are six boys in our class . . .

Eye color

VENN DIAGRAM	COLUMN GRAPH	PICTURE GRAPH	PIE CHART	LINE GRAPH

Extension Activity: Go through the newspaper and find examples of graphs. Label them and paste them into your math workbook.

Name	**Date**

1. Place a white sticker around the middle of a hexagonal pencil. Color three sides of the sticker blue and three yellow.

    a. Predict what color will be on top if you roll the pencil.

    b. Roll the pencil and see if you were right.

    c. Roll the pencil 12 times, predicting the answer before each roll. Keep a record of your answers on a separate piece of paper.

    d. Write a statement about what happened. _____

    _____

2. Begin again, but this time color two sides of the sticker blue, two sides yellow and two sides black.

    a. Roll the pencil 12 times, predicting the answer before each roll. Keep a record of your answers on a separate piece of paper.

    b. Write a statement about what happened. _____

    _____

3. This time, instead of using colors, write a different number on each of the six sides of the sticker.

    a. Roll the pencil 12 times, predicting the answer before each roll. Keep a record of your answers.

    b. Write a statement about what happened.

    _____

    _____

4. a. Which of the above spinners give you a 1:2 chance of predicting the right answer?

    _____

    b. Which of the above spinners give you a 1:3 chance of predicting the right answer?

    _____

    c. Which of the above spinners give you the greatest chance of predicting the right answer? _____

Extension Activity: Write a fairy tale in which the hero of the story must experience every one of a spinner's options.

(97)

Name	**Date**

For the following activities, use playing cards from 1 (Ace) to 9.

1. Take three different playing cards.

    a. Guess how many three-digit numbers it is possible to make with the three cards and write your guess in the box provided.

    b. List the possibilities on a sheet of paper and write the actual number (real amount) in the box provided.

    c. How close were you to the correct number?

Guess ☐

Actual ☐

Difference ☐

2. Now take four different playing cards.

    a. Guess how many four-digit numbers it is possible to make and write your guess in the box provided.

    b. List the possibilities on a sheet of paper and write the actual number (real amount) in the box provided.

    c. How close were you to the correct number?

Guess ☐

Actual ☐

Difference ☐

3. Again using the four cards, find out how many:

    a. three-digit numbers you can make from the four cards. _____

    b. two-digit numbers you can make from four cards. _____

4. **a.** Using the patterns from Question 1 and Question 2, predict how many one-digit numbers you can make from the four cards. _____

    b. Test your prediction. _____

    c. How close were you? _____

True or False?

Using patterns can help solve problems. However, we always need to check to be really sure.

Name	**Date**

1. On a separate piece of paper, write down your name and the names of your friends. Use first names and last names.

   Place the letters used under each letter of the alphabet in Table One.

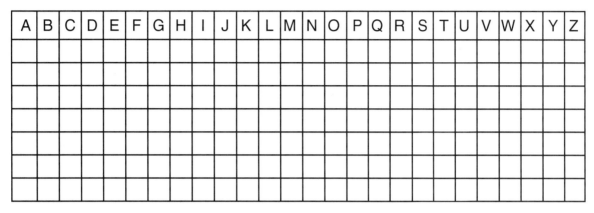

A	B	C	D	E	F	G	H	I	J	K	L	M	N	O	P	Q	R	S	T	U	V	W	X	Y	Z

   Write the number of letters you have in each column of Table One in Table Two below.

A	B	C	D	E	F	G	H	I	J	K	L	M	N	O	P	Q	R	S	T	U	V	W	X	Y	Z

   a. **Mean: The average number in a set of numbers.**

   How many letters did you use altogether?

   To find the mean you need to add the numbers in Table Two and divide the total by 26.

   _____ = This number is the **mean** (average) number of usage per letter.

   b. **Mode: The most common number in a set of numbers.**

   Which letter is the most **common**, or which number is written the most, in Table Two?

   _____ = This number is the **mode** of your results.

   c. **Median: When the numbers are in order of smallest to largest the median number is the middle number.**

   On the line below, place all the numbers from Table Two. Do not use zeros, but use repeat numbers in order from smallest to largest.

   _____

   Starting at number 1, find the middle number.

   _____ = This number is the **median** of your results.

Note: If there is no middle number, then take the two middle numbers, add them together, and divide this number in half. This number is your median.

99

Name	**Date**

1. Circle the answer.

    a. True or **False**   When you roll a die, there is a 1:6 chance of rolling a 4.

    b. True or **False**   When you toss a coin, there is a 1:1 chance it will land on heads.

    c. True or **False**   There are five ways to make ten cents using five cent and ten cent coins.

    d. True ort **False** With a deck of cards there is a 1:4 chance that any card you pick out will be from the hearts suit.

2. **Data:** There are twelve people in our class. Three people like chocolate milkshakes. The rest like strawberry milkshakes.

    Use this data to draw a column graph and a pie graph.

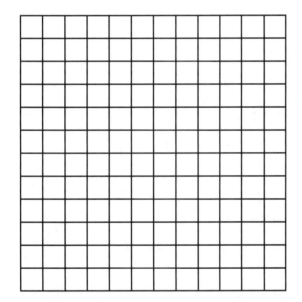
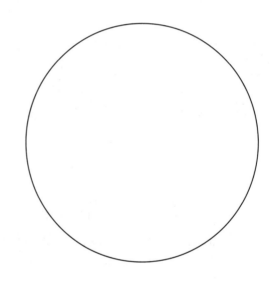

3. By looking at the graph to the right, you will see that it tells a story. What do you think the graph story might be about? Write a short story that matches what is shown in the graph. Use the back of this page.

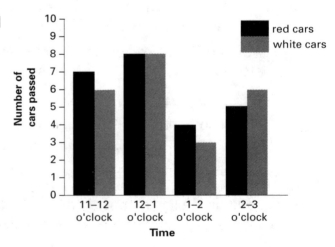

Name	**Date**

Predictions

1. Eight elephants were having races beside the river.

    a. When Elmo raced Elvie, the probability of Elmo winning was   _____ = ____

    b. When Exon raced Emmy, the probability of Exon winning was   _____ = ____

    c. When Elton raced Eric, the probability of Elton winning was   _____ = ____

    d. When Egbert raced Eddy, the probability of Egbert winning was   _____ = ____

    e. The chance of predicting four winners $: \frac{1}{2} \times \frac{1}{2} \times \frac{1}{2} \times \frac{1}{2} =$ _____

                                                 : 1 chance in _____

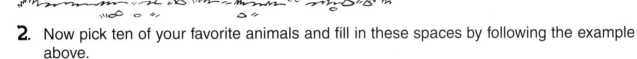

                                                 : a _____ to 1 chance

2. Now pick ten of your favorite animals and fill in these spaces by following the example above.

    a. When _____ raced _____ the probability of _____ winning was

        _____ = _____

    b. When _____ raced _____ the probability of _____ winning was

        _____ = _____

    c. When _____ raced _____ the probability of _____ winning was

        _____ = _____

    d. When _____ raced _____ the probability of _____ winning was

        _____ = _____

    e. When _____ raced _____ the probability of _____ winning was

        _____ = _____

    f. The chance of predicting four winners _____ : is __ x _____ x ____ x ___ x___ =

                                                   : is 1 chance in _____

                                                   : is a _____ to 1 chance

3. Try this exercise using 14 (or 20) sporting teams in a competition.

4. Each animal has a 50% chance of winning its race.

    a. Is it easy to predict the winner of one race? _____

    b. Is it easy to predict the winners of five races? _____

    Why? _____

(101)

CHANCE AND DATA

Unit 2

Expressions
Possibility
Data Recording
Mean, Mode, Median,
Range
Graphs

Objectives

- place informal expressions of chance on a numerical scale
- make simple predictive statements about everyday events using the appropriate language of chance
- use lists and tables to ensure all possibilities are considered
- revise a survey question so that it can be answered by yes/no or by a choice from a number of alternatives
- prepare a short questionnaire to enable data collection
- choose an appropriate graphical display with which to represent data
- use simple fractions and decimal fractions to summarize data
- calculate the mean and find the mode, median, and range of a data set
- display, read, and interpret a variety of graphs

Language

chance, data, all language of probability, numerical expression, occurrence, survey, tally, frequency, proportion, mean, mode, median, range, statistics, respondent

Materials/Resources

pens, paper, colored pencils

Contents of Student Pages

* *Materials needed for each reproducible student page*

Page 104 Chance
using terminology and expressions of chance; matching terms and expressions with events

Page 105 Possibilities
creating diagrams and formula for determining possibilities; for example—How many ways can you arrange the trophies on the shelf?

Page 106 Data Collection
writing questions; making predictions about results

Page 107 Recording Data
answering questions; checking predictions

* *colored pencils*

Page 108 Problem Solving
analyzing data using mean, mode, median, and range; determining which one is the most useful for a set of data

Page 109 Reading Data
making inferences from recorded data

Page 110 Assessment

Remember

- ❑ Problem solving strategies such as creating diagrams or tables correlate with chance and data problems.

Additional Activities

❏ *During everyday activities in the classroom, allow students to consider the likelihood of success.*

❏ *Have students keep records of their scores in various skills tests. Compute mean, median, mode, and range. Discuss the results with individual children so that they understand what this means about their performances.*

❏ *Use data from newspapers to provide useful discussion material on current events.*

Answers

Page 104 Chance

1. certain = high chance, probable = possible, even chance = fifty-fifty chance, low chance = unlikely, no chance = impossible
2. a. 1/12, 2/15, 1/5, 1/2, 2/3, 4/5, 7/8, 1/1 = 5/5
   b. unlikely = 1/12, 2/15, 1/5
      even chance = 1/2
      likely = 2/3, 4/5, 7/8, 19/20
      certain = 1/1, 5/5
3. a. h
   b. g
   c. f
   d. j
   e. i
4. b

Page 105 Possibilities

1. a. SMA, SAM, MSA, MAS, AMS, ASM
   b. IPFV, IPVF, IVPF, IVFP, IFPV, IFVP, PIFV, PIVF, PVIF, PVFI, PFVI, PFIV, VPFI, VPIF, VIPF, VIFP, VFPI, VFIP, FPVI, FPIV, FVIP, FVPI, FIPV, FIVP
2. a. 24 = 4 x 3 x 2 x 1
   b. 5 x 4 x 3 x 2 x 1 = 120

Page 106 Data Collection

1. Check individual work.
2. a, d
3. Check individual work.
4. Check individual work.
5. Check individual work.

Page 107 Recording Data

1. a. column graph
   b. pie chart
   c. line graph
   d. line graph
   e. bar graph (answers may vary)
2. Check individual work.
3. Check individual work.

Page 108 Problem Solving

1. a. 6
   b. 7
   c. 7
   d. 3
   e. 1 to 6
2. a. Rob: Mean = 9.5, Median = 8, Mode = 8
      Doug: Mean = 8:6, Median = 9, Mode = 9
   b. Rob
   e. Doug
   d. Doug
   e. Check individual work.
3. a. sizes of shoes
   b. range and Mode
   c. height of people
   d. mode
   e. ages of sixth grade children
   f. range

Page 109 Reading Data

1. a. 50
   b. 35
   c. 39
   d. 2%
   e. 10-50
   f. No
   g. b, c, d
2. a. Range
   b. What is the age group in which most people get their driver's licenses?
   c. Mean

Page 110 Assessment

1. b
2. 6 x 5 x 4 x 3 x 2 x 1 = 720 ways.
3. a
4. a. Whallop
   b. Blox
   c. Fielding
   d. 16
   e. column graph

Name

Date

1. The following terms express varying degrees of chance. Place them in order from most likely to least likely. Place an = sign between those that name equivalent expressions.

> even chance, no chance, certain, possible, probable, small chance,
> high chance, low chance, likely, unlikely, impossible, fifty-fifty chance

_____

_____

> Numerical expressions can also be given to express chance. The number of successes in relation to the total number of chances is the expression for the likelihood of the event occurring, for example—one chance in ten $\left(\frac{1}{10}\right)$ has less chance of happening that one chance in five $\left(\frac{1}{5}\right)$.

2. a. Place the following numerical expressions in order of likelihood from least likely to most likely. $\frac{1}{5}, \frac{2}{3}, \frac{7}{8}, \frac{1}{12}, \frac{1}{2}, \frac{4}{5}, \frac{2}{15}, \frac{1}{1}, \frac{19}{20}, \frac{5}{5}$

_____

b. Now place each numerical expression of chance in an appropriate box.

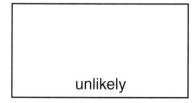

unlikely

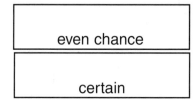

even chance

certain

likely

3. Match the following events with a suitable numerical expression from the left.

a. $\frac{1}{6}$ **f.** The next baby born will be a boy.

b. $\frac{1}{100}$ **g.** I will take the only pink ticket in a bag of 100 tickets.

c. $\frac{1}{2}$ **h.** You will throw a 3 with a regular die.

d. $\frac{1}{4}$ **i.** I will pull a 2 of clubs from a regular pack of cards.

e. $\frac{1}{52}$ **j.** You will pick a red sock from a bag of 5 red and 15 gray socks.

4. Circle one of the following events which has more than a fifty-fifty chance of happening tomorrow?

a. The next traffic light you see will be red.

b. You will put on clean clothes.

c. Lightning will strike your home.

(104)

Name	**Date**

All the possible ways that an event or occurrence can turn out are the **possibilities**. When tossing two coins, they could land as heads and heads, tails and tails, or heads and tails. There are three possibilities.

1. Using the codes given, show all the possibilities to arrange the following:

   a. Books on a shelf: Science (S), Math (M), Art (A)

   Example:

S M A		

   b. Plants on the patio: Ivy (I), Palm (P), Fern (F), Violet (V)

   Example:

I P F V		

2. There were six possibilities to arrange three books. 6 = 3 x 2 x 1

   a. There were 24 possibilities to arrange four plants. Following the pattern above, complete 24 = 4 x _____ x _____ x _____

   b. How many possibilities will there be to arrange five items on the clothes line?

   5 x _____ x _____ x _____ x _____ = _____

(105)

Name	**Date**

Scientists carry out research to discover data about various phenomena. They begin by posing questions about the phenomena. What questions do they ask?

1. Write two open-ended questions you could ask to determine the popularity of various entertainments among your classmates.

What? _____

How long? _____

2. Draw a checkmark next to any of the following that are yes/no questions.

   a. Do you read a newspaper?   **c.** When did you last have a vacation?

   b. What time do you leave for school?   **d.** Do you participate in a sport?

3. Think of some favorite pastimes that you could list as options for a survey. Use your list with the following questions. Anyone who answers the questions (including you!) has to use one of the options as an answer.

   a. Which of these is your favorite pastime? _____

   b. Which activity, apart from sleep, do you spend the most time doing? _____

_____

4. Ask 20 friends or classmates the questions from Question 3. Complete a frequency table for the results.

Recreation	Tally	Frequency

Recreation	Tally	Frequency

5. **a.** Write a yes/no question about travel. _____

   b. Write a set of choices to give a survey respondent about means of travel.

_____

Name	**Date**

Here are two ways to record data.

Table

	Cats	Dogs
Jo	2	0
Bill	1	2
Ted	2	3

Graph

---

1. Use colors to match the research topics with the most suitable graphs to use. Collect examples of these graph types from magazines or newspapers and discuss them.

   a. results of a fundraising campaign   line graph
   b. proportion of class-members who play main sports   pie chart
   c. progress of a cyclist   column graph
   d. growth of business profits   line graph
   e. proportion of total car production of each color choice   bar graph

2. **a.** Record the following information about work hours in a table to make reference to the information easier.

   In July, weeks 1–4, Bob worked 38 hours, 42 hours, 40 hours, and 39 hours; Sam worked 36 hours, 40 hours, 37.5 hours and 38.5 hours; Pedro worked 39 hours, 40 hours, 41.5 hours, and 39.5 hours.

	Week 1	Week 2	Week 3	Week 4	Totals
Bob					
Sam					
Pedro					

   b. Who would create this table? _____ Why? _____

3. Choose a topic related to travel about which to survey your teachers. What do you think you will find out? _____

   Write down your questions, make predictions about the information you will collect, tally answers, add frequencies, record results using the appropriate graph or table, and display your graph. Title of graph: _____

   Survey Questions: _____

   _____

Name	**Date**

To answer questions, we analyze data. This means summarizing and interpreting.

1. a. **Mean** refers to the average. The mean of 3, 7 and 8 is _____.

    b. **Median** refers to the middle number of a series when placed in order. The median of 2, 5, 7, 8 and 9 is _____.

    c. When there is an even number of numerals, the median is the average of the middle two. The median of 3, 4, 6, 8, 10 and 12 is _____.

    d. **Mode** refers to the number that occurs most often in a set of data. The mode of these scores 3, 2, 2, 4, 3, 6, 1, 3, and 1 is _____.

    e. **Range** refers to the range from the lowest to the highest data. The range in **d** is _____.

2. a. Complete the following data.

Scores in Gold Medal Shoot-off

										Mean	Median	Mode
Rob Shootalot	8	9	8	10	7	9	8	10	8	9			
Doug Deadeye	9	8	10	9	8	7	10	7	9	9			

    b. Using **mean**, who is the winner? _____

    c. Using **median**, who is the winner? _____

    d. Using **mode**, who is the winner? _____

    e. Who do you think should be the winner? _____ Why? _____

    _____

3. What data will the following people require?

    Which statistic (**mean, mode, median, range**) will be *most useful* for each of them?

Everyday event	Data Required	Most Useful Statistic
A shoe manufacturer needs to order sizes.	a.	b.
A mattress manufacturer needs to know how long to make mattresses.	c.	d.
A school principal needs to fill out a form showing oldest and youngest sixth-grade students' ages.	e.	f.

Name	**Date**

1. Study the graph of grammar test results. Answer the questions.

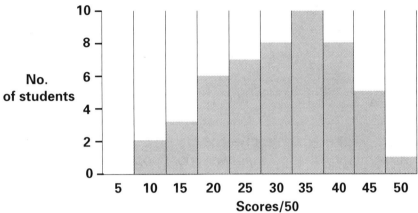

a. How many students took the test?   _____

b. What is the modal score?   _____

c. How many children passed the test with 100%?   _____

d. What percentage of students scored over 90% on the test?   _____

e. What is the range of scores?   _____

f. Did most students find the test difficult?

g. Circle the following questions which cannot be answered by this graph.

    a. How many students failed this test?   c. Which questions need revising?

    b. Which questions were well done?   d. Were girls the best performers?

2. Complete the table of everyday events, data required, and statistics most useful for analyzing the data.

Everyday Event	**Data Required**	**Most Useful Statistic**
Who are the oldest and youngest Olympians to win gold?	The age of Olympians who win gold medals.	a.
b.	Age group in which most people passed their driver's license test.	Mode
What is the age of a typical sixth-grade student?	Ages of all sixth-grade students.	c.

#8999 Targeting Math: Geometry, Chance, and Data

Name	**Date**

1. Circle the statement that has the greatest likelihood of happening:

   a. You draw a winning ticket in a raffle of 8 tickets.

   b. You choose a red marble from a sack of 2 red, 4 green, and 2 yellow.

   c. Throwing two dice, the resulting number will be a total of 1.

2. How many ways is it possible to arrange 6 items side by side on a shelf?

   _____

3. A class of children graphed their favorite ice cream choices. Vanilla was less popular than Mango swirl. Mango swirl was most popular. Lime was more popular than chocolate. Chocolate was least popular. Which graph shows this information?

   a.
   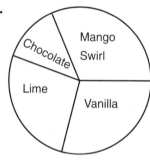

   b. Lime
   Vanilla
   Chocolate
   Mango Swirl

   c.

Choc	Lime	Vanilla	Mango Swirl

4. From the following table, answer the questions.

	Batting Scores
Sloggs	2, 8, 10, 15, 22, 26, 32
Whallop	8, 13, 15, 16, 16, 16, 46
Blox	0, 2, 5, 17, 20, 20, 22
Fielding	4, 5, 8, 10, 22, 25, 45

   a. Whose average score is the best? _____

   b. Who has the least range in scores? _____

   c. Using median scores, who has the lowest score?_____

   d. Whallop has a modal score of _____

   e. Which type of graph would best represent this information?_____

Skills Index

The following index lists specific objectives for the student pages of each unit in the book. The objectives are grouped according to the sections listed in the Table of Contents. Use the Skills Index as a resource for identifying the units and student pages you wish to use.

Three-Dimensional Shapes

recognize three-dimensional objects (Page: 11)

describe three-dimensional objects (Page: 11)

make and represent three-dimensional objects (Page: 12)

identify prisms from drawings (Page: 8)

identify pyramids from drawings (Page: 9)

describe and compare faces, edges, and vertices of prisms (Page: 8)

describe and compare faces, edges, and vertices of pyramids (Page: 9)

make complex models from visual information (Pages: 12, 13)

represent three-dimensional shapes by drawing models (Page: 10)

draw recognizable cylinders, cones, and spheres (Pages: 19, 20)

sketch elevations of cones, cylinders, and spheres (Page: 19)

list properties of cones, cylinders, and spheres (Page: 18)

select figures that meet criteria related to sides, faces, and vertices (Page: 18)

recognize an object from different view points (Page: 21)

discuss packing properties of three-dimensional objects (Page: 19)

investigate and describe cross-sections of three-dimensional shapes (Page: 20)

Two-Dimensional Shapes

use degrees as a formal unit (Page: 29)

construct angles using a protractor (Pages: 30, 31)

read scales to the nearest measurement mark (Page: 28)

use conventional units and measuring equipment for angles (Pages: 28, 29, 30, 31, 32, 41)

examine properties of triangles (Page: 32)

examine properties of quadrilaterals (Pages: 38, 39, 40)

classify angles according to size (Page: 27)

use geometric tools to interpret and meet specifications (Pages: 39, 48, 49)

select figures that meet criteria (Pages: 37, 41)

classify polygons and other two-dimensional shapes (Pages: 37, 40)

describe and compare properties of two-dimensional shapes (Page: 40)

use conventional language associated with circles (Page: 48)

identify and describe horizontal and vertical lines (Page: 47)

describe and construct patterns (Pages: 47, 49)

use lines in pattern making (Page: 47)

use a compass (Page: 48)

select appropriate technology (Pages: 50, 51, 52)

construct polygons and other two-dimensional shapes (Pages: 50, 51, 52)

meet specifications requiring accurate constructions (Page: 51)

extend a mathematical investigation by asking questions (Page: 50)

Transformation

describe, construct, and interpret patterns (Page: 57)

describe, construct, and interpret patterns and tessellations (Page: 58)

recognize that objects can be represented using scale models (Page: 61)

#8999 Targeting Math: Geometry, Chance and Data

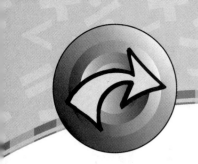

Skills Index

recognize that objects can be represented using scale models and make simple calculations using scale (Page: 59)

identify shapes with line symmetry (Page: 60)

construct and classify polygons and other two-dimensional shapes and describe and compare their patterns (Page: 62)

recognize, visualize, describe, make and represent three-dimensional objects (Page: 62)

Position and Mapping

use simple coordinates or compass points to mark out points on a grid (Pages: 68, 71, 72)

demonstrate a willingness to work cooperatively with others and to value the contributions of others (Pages: 67, 71)

appreciate the contribution of mathematics to our society (Page: 67)

give clear instructions for moving and finding objects on plans, using directions (Page: 67)

produce models, labeling key features of a location (Page: 71)

interpret maps (Pages: 71, 80)

find paths to satisfy specifications (Pages: 70, 79)

describe and label the position of objects in relation to one another (Pages: 68, 72)

use mathematical terminology and some conventions to explain, interpret and represent position (Pages: 69, 70, 79)

use simple coordinates to describe position and marks out points on a grid (Pages: 77, 78)

produce maps, labeling key features of a location (Page: 80)

follow and describe location and paths using distance and direction (Page: 80)

Chance and Data

interpret data (Pages: 96, 99)

display, read, and interpret a variety of graphs (Pages: 86, 87, 88, 89, 90, 91, 92, 94, 95, 107, 109)

compare different representations of the same data (Page: 88)

recognize the economy and power of mathematical notation, terminology and convention in helping to develop and communicate mathematical ideas (Page: 99)

represent, interpret, and explain mathematical situations using everyday language with some mathematical terminology, including simple graphs and diagrams (Page: 85)

pose questions and collect data (Pages: 85, 86)

contribute to discussions to clarify which data would help answer particular questions or test predictions, and take care in collecting data (Page: 86)

take care in collecting data (Page: 86)

appreciate the impact of mathematical information on daily life (Page: 86)

record and identify all possible outcomes arising from chance experiments (Page: 98)

consider predictions after data collections (Pages: 97, 98)

place informal expressions of chance on a numerical scale (Page: 104,)

make simple predictive statements about everyday events using the appropriate language of chance (Page: 104)

use lists and tables to ensure all possibilities are considered (Page: 105)

revise a survey question so that it can be answered by yes/no or by a choice from a number of alternatives (Page: 106)

prepare a short questionnaire to enable data collection (Page: 106)

choose an appropriate graphical display with which to represent data (Page: 107)

calculate the mean and find the mode and median, and range of a data set (Pages: 108, 109)

#8999 Targeting Math: Geometry, Chance and Data